THE
CHEMISTRY
FACTOR

CREATE
POWERFUL BUSINESS RELATIONSHIPS
FOR GREATER SUCCESS

THE
CHEMISTRY
FACTOR

CREATE
POWERFUL BUSINESS RELATIONSHIPS
FOR GREATER SUCCESS

BARNEY FEINBERG

REDSEAMS PUBLISHING

NEW YORK

Published by RedSeams Publishing
Printed in the United States of America

Cover Design by Ryan K. Fishman

ISBN 978-1-7321625-0-1 (paperback)
ISBN 978-1-7321625-1-8 (ebk)

This book is dedicated to my Mom and Dad –
who brought me up to be
open-minded, inclusive, and caring.

TABLE OF CONTENTS

LIST OF EXERCISES

Discover the Values of Others

Ignite Authentic Connection

FOREWORD

"There are always people I can't stand." What do I actually mean when I say this?

Well, maybe it's the way they express themselves. Or maybe it's the substance of what they say. Whatever it is, the effort it takes me to communicate with them isn't worth the trouble because in the end I'm left with nothing but frustration.

So when my friend Barney Feinberg approached me to be a critical reader for his new book, *The Chemistry Factor*, I resisted. I didn't want to make the effort to get to know people I'd already determined were lost causes. Then, when Barney asked me to be a test client for his Chemistry Factor coaching, I really dug my heels in.

When I ultimately agreed, Barney then trotted out all these values he said I might have. I resisted even further. I was perfectly happy with the few values I thought I had. They worked for me. Why expand them as a basis to get to know people I had already determined I didn't want to get to know!

It was only after the first session or two that I began to see Barney's wisdom. By identifying more and more values that I in fact had, I was able to expand my values potential, or Chemistry Factor. It became worthwhile to revisit these people I had rejected because I "had no use" for them. Lo and behold, common values emerged as I identified more and more values I had. Uninteresting or off-putting people became interesting and attractive because they and I had values in common.

Now when I come up blank in an initial conversation with someone, I run down my values list in my mind and seek common ground. It usually emerges.

Barney presents his program as a way to build powerful business networks, and it certainly is that. However, I've found it's much more – it's a way to make friends I never would have given a second's notice to, just because I've expanded my own capacity to do so by fully knowing how widely inclusive my values are.

I've urged Barney to follow up *The Chemistry Factor* with a more comprehensive work that explores how the encouragement to use widely shared values might help improve understanding and peace in the world. His approach certainly has this potential.

– Wayne Caskey
Executive coach for seventeen years
Former CEO & C-level executive at two Fortune 500 enterprises

ACKNOWLEDGMENTS

I would like to acknowledge the many business associates, family, and friends who have encouraged me to write this book over the last five years: the business associates whose faith in my coaching program supported me through the journey to reach completion; my family who kept me on my path through encouragement and trust; and the many friends who, by asking repeatedly when it would be finished, kept inspiring me to complete it.

Empowering my values of confidence, joy, and enthusiasm reinforced my writing journey and direction. The gifts of new values that presented themselves in the process of writing this book, often unexpectedly, inspired my values of discovery and creativity, which fueled my motivation.

Special thanks to my wife, Tracey; my son, Aaron; and my daughter, Joelle, who fill my life with love; to Wayne Caskey for his powerful listening and masterful coaching; and to Sakada, my book coach, for her persistence and dedication to my success.

YOUR CHEMISTRY FACTOR

ONE

GREAT CHEMISTRY

Whether you're a CEO, an entrepreneur, or in your first job out of college, you have experienced success. I have coached people who asked me, "Why does work feel less inspiring than it used to?" Others find themselves in stop-and-go action, constantly navigating what seems to be company politics to the detriment of their productivity. Then there are others who continually climb their ladders of success but wonder why it feels like such hard work, paddling upstream.

The Chemistry Factor will answer these questions and many others you might have about taking your success to the next level by inspiring you to take actions that create stronger business relationships, quickly and easily.

> *The most important single ingredient*
> *in the formula of success is knowing*
> *how to get along with people.*
> — Theodore Roosevelt

David, a client services director, was sizzling mad as he walked back to his office after being handed his head on a platter by the owner and CEO of the boutique advertising agency he was working for. "This guy is impossible to deal with. One day he's your best friend and the next day he hates you."

This was the atmosphere that David worked in, and he got plenty of affirmation from the people he worked with about how bad the chemistry his CEO created was – except from one person.

Paul was the CFO – the CEO's business partner. They spent a lot of time together. The CEO was never seen to get into a fight or be upset with Paul. People thought the CEO avoided getting angry with him because Paul must know where all the bodies were buried in this agency. But he had only been with the agency for a short time, just under two years – one year less than David.

The CFO before Paul, who had been there much longer, had been a whipping boy for this CEO, often berated. He left the agency, it was said, because he couldn't take it anymore. What was Paul's secret? How could he deal with this man who constantly ran hot and cold with everyone else?

One day in a senior management meeting, the CEO was livid about overspending on a project that had not been approved by the client. David shifted his focus to Paul, expecting he would finally get some fire. He saw that Paul's demeanor was no different from when he had walked into the meeting. Paul was listening intently to the CEO rant, but seemed calm, cool, and collected. Just looking at Paul made the anger coming from the CEO look less intimidating to David.

As the CEO cooled down, David realized that Paul had not reacted like everyone else had to the anger being vented in the meeting. Some were angry, and others were afraid. But Paul was not allowing the circumstances to dictate how he reacted. He was calm, giving anger and fear no place to go but out.

After the meeting, David took Paul aside and asked him why the CEO never directed his anger toward him. Paul said, "My being upset does not help the situation." He had learned that allowing someone's frustration and anger to cause him to get angry clouds the conversation and is counterproductive to solving the issue.

Paul added, "Knowing that he's getting his point across to me gives him the confidence that I will rectify the situation. Being angry and afraid when he's angry only breeds more upset. He's told me I'm one of the few people he connects with; I know how to calm him down." By connecting to his value of listening powerfully to the details of the conversation and focusing on the content of what is being said and not the emotion, Paul isn't affected by the upset and the CEO feels powerfully heard, which is what he really wants.

In business, we often allow circumstances to dictate who we are being by reacting rather than choosing who we want to be no matter what the circumstances. When I ask people if they've ever had a stressful relationship at work, they all tell me yes. Just asking the question can make someone re-live the stress and discomfort that a bad relationship creates. Poor relationship chemistry at work has us overthink and underperform, and triggers the anger or upset that leads to poor business decisions.

When I speak of chemistry in this book, I refer to the interaction between people who work together; specifically, the type of interaction that is harmonious and effective. Your *Chemistry Factor* is your ability to powerfully interact with and connect to values you have in common with the people at work, creating effective, authentic relationships.

This book shows you how to create a great business relationship with *anyone* in your company. Building great relationships at work is the primary inspiration for igniting the chemistry that inspires greater business success.

We all know people who use their Chemistry Factor successfully: the entrepreneur who attracts the best strategic talent to the company because he plays in a big-picture vision with others; the CEO who by encouraging camaraderie is as welcome in the production room as the boardroom; the creative director who powerfully connects with her colleagues in client services because she is a strong listener who understands her clients' expectations.

Executives with a strong Chemistry Factor bring great passion to any company. Productivity, and the resulting profitability, is high due to their ability to authentically connect with everyone and anyone at work. They know how to consciously create chemistry in their business relationships. When you are with them, you are seen, heard, appreciated, and inspired. You strive for more of their enrolling personality and ease of action in the workplace, but too often the steps you take to reach your goals feel like hard work, and you have only excuses as to why. When an executive's Chemistry Factor is fired up they are ready to go. It's time to stop waiting – you can fire up your chemistry, too!

CHEMISTRY IGNITES

Let's talk about chemistry.

"Connection chemistry," while intangible, is a factor in your success and happiness. It is the chemistry that elevates and empowers your relationships with others.

Let's be clear. I'm not talking about the science of elements, compounds, and substances. I'm not talking about blowing things up in high school science lab. I'm talking about the spark of chemistry that ignites your business relationships – the rapport, understanding, and true engagement that lifts your work performance and that of those you connect with. When your Chemistry Factor is high, your approach to work is naturally more powerful and enrolling.

UNDERSTANDING CHEMISTRY

A few more distinctions about the chemistry we are talking about in this book:

COUPLES CHEMISTRY V. BUSINESS CHEMISTRY

Having chemistry in a personal relationship usually refers to love and intimacy. This book is not about that type of chemistry. *The Chemistry Factor* will show you how to create "spark-inspired" business connections. You will find that since you spend a tremendous amount of your waking hours at work, the more people you can spark chemistry with, the more satisfying your work life will be.

GOOD AND BAD CHEMISTRY

Though there are, of course, instances in which people call the chemistry "bad" and the interaction feels dysfunctional, when discussing Chemistry-Factor chemistry, we will direct to the good chemistry – the chemistry that comes from authentic connection.

I had the pleasure of working with a well-respected client account director of a large advertising agency in New York City. Carol (not her real name) understood how to authentically connect with the people at work. She loved challenging her staff to go beyond the expected to achieve excellence. For some who were new to the firm, her approach made them feel concerned that they were not achieving better results fast enough. Then they got to know her.

She held herself to the same standards of excellence. Before clients came to the office she would work the same late hours, without complaint, and get excited when a marketing plan or program update was well prepared. Her motivation was infectious. She encouraged and acknowledged the staff's big and small successes and promoted advancement for those who gave the extra effort. They saw her as a mentor and would go out of their way to support her.

Those who worked with Carol made a point of maintaining their relationships even after leaving the company. Many would socialize with her to catch up, share ideas on industry developments, or ask for career advice. Her ability to authentically connect with her staff through the value of acknowledgment brought with it great relationships and success; she was skilled at creating good chemistry.

THE CHEMISTRY IN YOUR FACTOR
QUICK CONNECTION IS GOOD

Through learning how to connect with people quickly, your Chemistry Factor allows you to stay connected with people more often. The more people you stay connected with, the better for your business and career.

If you have ever gotten angry at work, you know that it can consume your thinking. Being the elephant who never forgets can have you carrying the upset around like a martyr. Imagine how much greater your productivity at work can be when you quickly let go of what's upsetting you and reconnect with your coworkers.

THE WIN-WIN

The Chemistry-Factor approach is flexible, while also allowing you to stay true to who you are. This results in an ability to connect with a diverse group of people with greater inclusivity and mutual empowerment. Everyone wins.

Perhaps there was a time in your career when you wanted to brainstorm and the person you were working with wanted their independence. Drawing a line in the sand that says "My way or else" when this happens does not inspire either of you to greater success.

We all have values in common, and being able to connect to a common value you have with another, such as dedication, strengthens the relationship. You are still being true to who you are while not getting stuck in a disconnected relationship.

DEPTH = AUTHENTICITY

Depth brings ease and gravitas to the connection. When you can directly connect in caring and meaningful ways, your relationships expand to become more supportive, inspiring, and significant; they go from powerful to amazing.

Every value has a definition, but it is the depth of the story behind the value that connects us in a more significant way. I remember working many eighty-plus-hour work weeks to establish an overseas buying office in Hong Kong. I woke up every day looking forward to going to work, building a new business while experiencing dynamic growth. That memory gives my value of dedication greater depth. When I'm connecting with someone who appreciates that level of dedication, our productivity is inspiring.

EASY IS NATURAL

When you deeply connect to a value, you are *being* the value rather than thinking of being it. Your ability to embrace a value eventually becomes as easy as breathing air.

There was a managing director at a media agency who was having stressful conversations with one of his planning directors. The planning director was not a very good listener but was very good at managing the client's media metrics. The managing director wanted to be calm when speaking with her, but inside he was burning because he constantly had to repeat himself. He learned to empower the value of calm, and in so doing discovered that she began listening to him more powerfully. People can feel who you're being with them, even when you think they can't.

3 TYPES OF BUSINESS RELATIONSHIPS

Think about your business relationships. For each one, into which of the three following categories does it fall?

1. Stagnant: connected but expected – the relationship works but it's not growing. It can be cordial, but it's the same old same old without any spark.

2. Dysfunctional: rejected and disconnected – frustrating, with moments of explosion, working with this person is unnecessarily difficult and energy-draining!

3. On the Rise: innovative and inspiring – expansive with possibility and growth, this is the means by which great business relationships develop.

The greater danger for most of us lies
not in setting our aim too high and falling short;
but in setting our aim too low and achieving our mark.
—Michelangelo

Imagine all your business relationships were on the rise! What would it be like to continually build bridges of connection while watching the walls of disconnection crumble? For some of you this would be amazing; for others the mere thought makes you feel uncomfortable or overwhelmed.

In my work with thousands of executives I have found that those who are goal-oriented tend to focus on the finish line before they start the race, which can make any goal look overwhelming even when it isn't. The Chemistry-Factor approach addresses one relationship at a time, not all at once. You get to decide the pace and with whom you want to create great relationships. Rushing to a finish line is counterproductive.

YOUR CHEMISTRY FACTOR

Because your relationships with coworkers are key to the enthusiasm that breeds success, your ability to create great relationships, or your Chemistry Factor, is vital. It begins with one interaction and spreads, one person and one interaction at a time. Before you know it you have a network of strong, positive relationships.

How strong are your business relationships? It's likely you have a network of relationships. Some are your go-to relationships that you count on for support, while others make your business decisions and actions harder to reach because they do not reflect alignment between you and the other person.

Jason was the CEO and founding partner of a digital advertising agency. Over the course of the agency's four years in business it had grown from three partners to over 60 staff. The agency was run from the top down by millennials who had great ideas and were enthusiastic, but lacked sophisticated management experience. This led to communication problems between departments and staff members in important areas of timely deliverables and operational oversight.

Jason was the new business and strategy guru. He was responsible for bringing in the agency's big clients with his strategic thinking and enrolling personality. However, as the business expanded he was thrown into the problems that continually developed in operations. This was a responsibility Jason did not enjoy. He would get angry, undermine the authority of others out of frustration, and place blame out loud in front of the management team.

It became clear that Jason had developed a trust issue with most everyone in the company, using his valuable time to micromanage others. He was not happy, nor were his partners and the staff. He decided to use the Chemistry Factor to reset his relationships.

Realizing that he was making others wrong by being disconnected from the value of trust, he looked for other values he had in common with those he worked with. To do this he first built greater self-awareness of his values, identifying, defining, and consciously empowering them using the Chemistry-Factor technique. This was eye-opening for Jason. As is true of most of us, his value perspectives were more often instinctive and not consciously chosen.

Jason began working from new value perspectives that his partners and staff could connect to, such as mentoring, having a sense of humor, and strategic thinking, to name a few. Being more mindful of his values made it possible for him to identify in conversation the values he had in common with others at work as well as those they did not have in common.

It did not take long for Jason to implement his Chemistry-Factor skills. An important media-buy and insertion was incorrectly authorized, without client approval. Jason immediately called for a management meeting to make right what had gone wrong. Expecting the worst, people in the conference room were anxious and defensive. But instead of telling others what went wrong with a demeaning tone, Jason started with some sarcastic wit. With a straight face he asked the team who could lend him the money to cover the overspend – he would pay them back next week.

The silence in the room turned to smiles as Jason began to grin. Everyone seemed to breathe a collective sigh of relief, and with it a great deal of tension left the room. He then proceeded to ask for advice about how to prevent such a problem from happening again in the future. His senior managers enthusiastically shared their thoughts and worked together to come up with an answer that had universal support.

They improved the communication flow between the client services and project management teams to avoid repeating the same problem in the future. Jason then reached out to the client to explain the issue and take responsibility for the overspend. The agreed resolution cost the agency money but also forged a stronger client relationship.

Jason overcame his frustration and anger by empowering the values he shared with his coworkers. He strived to become a delegator instead of a dictator. Then trust became a value he could empower with his team, and they became inspired to make sure it was earned. This strengthening of relationships resulted in the agency surpassing that year's sales goals within the first six months of the year.

When you are authentically connected in your business relationships, your odds for success are limitless, and everything is possible.

The focus of this book is on using the Chemistry Factor with your coworkers up and down the company structure.

While *The Chemistry Factor* was written to help you work within your company, you will also notice that your Chemistry Factor is a huge asset in working with your customers and your network outside your company.

TWO

AUTHENTIC CONNECTION

A technology director in a digital media agency made a point of avoiding the head of client services. His efforts to stay clear of her were at times exhausting, and the struggle made him question whether to stay with the dynamic agency he otherwise enjoyed working for.

He loved tailoring tech to all departments, but was not the best at communicating the process to people who did not speak the language. The lack of clear communication created a lot of frustration and finger-pointing when the project-management information failed to meet expectations.

Every day the technology director prepared himself for more frustrating conversations with client services, until he discovered that one of his younger managers had started his career in client services and could make the dashboard process easy for them to understand.

The tech director was a proud man who wanted to lead communications with all departments but realized that by honoring the value of delegation he could have this young manager better explain how the system worked.

The head of client services saw the delegation for communication as a stroke of powerful leadership that made everybody's work more efficient and less stressful. The tech director now had more time to engineer better systems that were appreciated by all in the company.

The key to building a successful career lies in your ability to create great business relationships. These connections do not always start off smoothly. Some people might not seem worth the energy, you might not be in the mood, or you might feel you have better things to do with your time than struggle to achieve a good relationship with them. Regardless, each person in your company is worthy of a meaningful working relationship.

This book focuses on one-on-one authentic connection, but using the Chemistry Factor with groups of people is also powerful. Naturally, as you master one-on-one authentic connection, your skill working with groups of people improves as well. It starts with one relationship.

THE POWER OF AUTHENTIC CONNECTION

You have experienced authentic connection: *the matching of a value you have in common with someone else at the same time*. It occurs when you are listening rather than just hearing, working on the same wavelength they are on rather than just sitting next to them, or embracing a challenge in the relationship rather than just going through the motions. It is when "have to" becomes "want to," and time is no longer a linear affair. It is when there are no deadlines – just the goal and the journey to the destination.

The relationship between Microsoft's Bill Gates and The Oracle of Omaha, Warren Buffet, is an amazing example of the power of authentic connection. They are two of the richest men in the world who developed a great relationship despite what initially seemed to both as their having nothing in common and being total opposites. As read in a story written by Bill Gates (see https://www.gatesnotes.com/About-Bill-Gates/25-Years-of-Learning-and-Laughter), Bill was a tech nerd and Warren was an investor who didn't use email.

When they first met on July 5th, 1991, there was an immediate camaraderie that continues to blossom. Bill credits this in part to Warren's ability to "invest in people." When Bill and Warren speak about their relationship, many of the values they have in common are identified. Their sense of humor, thirst for knowledge, brainstorming, mentoring, and kindness are but some of the values that connect them.

As successful as they are, their relationship took their success to even greater levels. Bill and Warren are passionate philanthropists. Together they created a paradigm shift in giving when Bill was creating his charity foundation. The shift was to envision the act of charity as taking on the same dynamic in fighting poverty and disease as software had in building business success. They used technology and its developmental techniques to magnify and speed up charitable success. Today they are two of the greatest philanthropists in the world.

When you remember some of the best experiences you've had – moments when you felt totally alive and true to yourself, you are identifying instances of connection with yourself: the presentation you gave to win that new client, the white paper you wrote that helped build your personal brand, or the last point of a tennis match you won in a tie-breaker.

If you then remember sharing the same deep, true moments with others, you are recognizing points of connection with them. These peak moments came to you naturally, and you experienced them as both intangible and very physically real.

Think also about the moments of authentic connection you have witnessed. For example, the authentic connection that manifests between teammates in sports is a sight to behold.

I remember the USA hockey team in the 1980 Olympics. Their magical victory to win the gold medal will be forever remembered as a peak moment signifying a great accomplishment. Yet the event that to this day still inspires me was during the award ceremony when the whole team climbed onto the gold medal podium. It was a spontaneous action, each player balanced without an extra inch of room to stand, and a testament to the powerful authentic relationships they developed together.

I've learned that people will forget what you said,
people will forget what you did, but people
will never forget how you made them feel.
—Maya Angelou

Points of authentic connection are keys to great business relationships. Those connections are working long after the last handshake, the affirmative "see you soon," or the email signoff. They are working 24/7, 365.

Meanwhile, beyond your personal experience, you can rest assured that study after study confirmed that being able to connect with others brings multiple benefits to one's career.

Leigh Branham is the owner of Keeping the People, Inc. and an expert in understanding employee turnover. He pointed out in his continuing professional education (CPE) course, published by Professional Education Services, LP, in February of 2015, that there are seven reasons employees leave a company. It is fair to equate at least three of them to poor business relationships:

1. Feeling devalued and unrecognized

2. Loss of trust and confidence in senior leaders

3. Too little coaching and feedback

When you authentically connect and create powerful business relationships with the people you work with, such issues improve dramatically and in turn address the other four reasons for staff turnover in a positive way:

4. Job not as expected

5. Mismatch of job and person

6. Too few growth opportunities

7. Stress from overwork and lack of balance between work life and personal life

IGNITE YOUR CHEMISTRY-FACTOR SUCCESS

Igniting the authenticity of your connections increases your success at all levels, from how you feel on a daily basis to increasing your company's bottom line. This is success that feels great in every way!

Your Chemistry Factor essentially powers up and improves your business and career, from your day-to-day work to your big-picture goals. Your Chemistry Factor positively affects your work life, your success as a leader, and your personal productivity.

YOUR CHEMISTRY-FACTOR WORK LIFE

The TGI Friday person doesn't know how to make their work weeks as real and significant in their life as their weekends. They box each one separately. Work is, well… work. You can only hope they have a great weekend planned, because those forty-plus hours spent too often disconnected from their values at work are a tough penance to pay.

Thanks to the Chemistry Factor, you will enjoy a more inspired approach to your work day. You will also have great weekends. In fact, you will have better weekends! But instead of separating your life from your work, both your work and your personal life will feel fulfilling and satisfying. TGI Friday will become TGI Monday, TGI Tuesday….

This is the difference that strengthening your Chemistry Factor will make.

YOUR CHEMISTRY-FACTOR LEADERSHIP
Confidence + Charisma = Leadership

As a coach of travel baseball and soccer for my children, I found it easy to notice the one thing that made all the difference in how children approach the game: confidence. When they were confident, their performance on the field improved dramatically. When teammates were confident in each other, they played brilliantly. Win or lose, they walked off the field knowing they gave their all and pumped up to play the next game.

When you are empowering your values on the field of business, you are playing your "A game." When you are authentically connected with your workmates on the field, your success is magnified. Learning how to consciously expand your Chemistry Factor brings you the extraordinary results you want for your company and career.

Believing in yourself, your abilities, and your talents inspires a greater level of leadership in you. That in turn ignites your natural charisma, compelling others to search you out for guidance and inspiration.

I remember working with a CFO who experienced great success until he left his firm to work with an exciting new start-up agency. Within a short time he realized it was a miscalculation on his part; the agency went belly up for lack of additional venture capital funding.

Many in his situation would have lost confidence in themselves. His mortgage was still due, his family was living an upper-middle-class lifestyle, and he had plans to vacation in Europe that month. But his confidence in himself made his path to a new position much easier. He walked into interviews with a can-do spirit and attitude as if he were still working. The people he met were very connected with him. By the time he returned from vacation he had a new job offer for more than he had been making, with a commute that improved his quality of life.

Your ability to quickly and easily make authentic connections with others creates a chain reaction that fires up your confidence and charisma. The more chemistry you generate with your Chemistry Factor, the better your relationships with coworkers are and the more others see you as a leader.

YOUR CHEMISTRY–FACTOR PRODUCTIVITY

Banging your head against the wall in frustration will not lead to greater productivity. If you find yourself on your own, staying late in the office every night, your productivity is calling for improvement.

I remember auditing a Hong Kong fashion-buying office for a leading clothing conglomerate in the USA which was in partnership with the office's Hong Kong parent company. For years the office was unable to report accurate financial statements, so the clothing company sent me over to investigate.

The local employees' loyalty was to the Hong Kong parent company, which made my audit search very difficult to complete. After months of investigating and working nonstop 80-hour-plus work weeks, I completed the audit, the partnership disbanded, and I was exhausted.

I was asked to stay on with the USA company, charged to set up its own buying office. Again, for several years, 80-hour-plus work weeks were common. Yet with a team of locals who worked with me rather than against me, the experience was invigorating. We outgrew our office space every six months, starting with a staff of five and building to 125 employees in five years' time. My energy soared and I assimilated into the culture, leaving after seven years with lifelong friendships.

Having authentically connected relationships with your coworkers improves your personal productivity while also enhancing your company's overall productivity.

IGNITE YOUR COMPANY SUCCESS

Your Chemistry Factor will not just fire up your personal success, but also ignite your company's culture and performance. No matter where someone is in the company structure, their use of the Chemistry Factor powerfully affects their coworkers, having a positive, cascading influence.

CHEMISTRY-FACTOR COMPANY CULTURE

A Chemistry-Factor company culture is one in which all employees enjoy their work and feel acknowledged and respected; where everyone is working at their best and succeeding individually and for the company as a whole.

There are many criteria that can be used to "measure" a company's culture. In regard to the Chemistry Factor, we aspire to an environment and culture that promotes employee inclusion and engagement.

Greater Employee Inclusion and Engagement

Employees work better and harder for a boss they believe in. Imagine the people you work with not only believing in you, but you believing in them as well.

When you are authentically connected with your coworkers, working relationships are much more fruitful. It builds an expanded feeling of inclusion and engagement among everyone in the office. These powerful relationships have a huge impact on the company culture in general.

Authentic Connection Leads to Inclusion

A company is bigger than any one person. Great things happen when your coworkers think in terms of "we" instead of "I." This is exactly what the Chemistry Factor brings to the game.

Kathy wanted to leave her new company after only six months. She was not fitting in with the people in her department; they put her in what felt like a sink-or-swim situation. The Chemistry Factor inspired her to give this new company another chance.

After three weeks of coaching, Kathy felt more connected with her coworkers. She found that when she shifted her attention from the value of focusing to get the work finished to the value of taking the time to listen to her coworkers, *they* listened to *her*, which resulted in her getting more done in less time. Six months later, when I told her about a job she might be interested in, she would not even consider leaving.

Being devalued and unrecognized is a major reason for poor company success and high employee turnover. Feeling like a part of the company and being included in conversations that get the work done are key benefits of the Chemistry Factor.

Authentic Connection Leads to Engagement

When coworkers feel heard, seen, valued, and respected,

they are more engaged. The Chemistry-Factor relationships you foster with your coworkers create these feelings.

Sean was hired as a social media director for an advertising agency that had limited talent in marketing social media for its clients. He came in as the expert who would get things done. This expectation fit well with his ability to see the forest above the trees in social media strategic planning; he was way ahead of everyone else on the subject.

That, however, is what caused the disconnect. His value of expediency, which he saw as expected from an expert, left everyone else behind. No one else on the team felt heard by him; he was moving too quickly, which is what he thought the client wanted, only to find that the client felt left behind as well.

He rarely, if ever, used patience in his work life. However, using the Chemistry-Factor approach, he recalled a peak moment when he had been with friends on a boat, fishing for flounder off Long Island, New York. There was no rush then; patience was a value appreciated by all. He was amazed to find that when he authentically connected with his work team from the value of patience, no one felt left behind and everyone became more engaged and productive, including him!

CHEMISTRY-FACTOR
COMPANY PERFORMANCE

A company filled with top-notch relationships is a company performing well on many levels. If the performance at your company needs a boost, Chemistry-Factor connection is the potent element that can quickly and dramatically raise the level of success. The big-picture benefits of this chemistry are innovation, productivity, and profitability.

More Innovation

When your coworkers feel your authenticity, they feel more comfortable being authentic themselves. This is possible when the relationships at your company work at a Chemistry-Factor level. This then leads to more creative thinking, and when each employee is approaching their work in this way, innovation happens almost miraculously.

Pamela described a snowball effect when her employees felt more and more comfortable about expressing their ideas to her and to each other. Once an attitude of openness took hold, her employees' problem-solving and project-planning became more creative and innovative. Innovation is inevitable when creative minds are unrestricted through an inclusive and engaged company dynamic.

More Productivity

Each Chemistry-Factor connection you make is a step up in your productivity. Start the addition and let it add up, remembering that the coworker on the other end of your connection is also increasing their productivity.

Implementing the Chemistry Factor in your interactions with coworkers sends productivity up because amazing business relationships tend to inspire everyone they touch. Best of all, productivity becomes contagious and infects everyone at the company.

More Profit

The bottom line is, of course, the bottom line. Profitability is a natural outcome when you work with others in authentic connection. Company culture has a great impact on company performance, and a productive one leads to greater profit.

My first Chemistry-Factor coaching client, Wayne Caskey, who wrote the foreword for this book, was a fellow business coach who worked with the highest of C-level executives throughout the world. He agreed to critique my program without any expectation of success. During the course of the program he told me that he would win an average of three to four new business accounts in a year. Within three months of working on his Chemistry Factor, he attained seven new accounts and had to stop taking on new business – a good problem to have.

YOUR CHEMISTRY-POWERED CAREER

You are reading this book because you know that activating your Chemistry Factor will make a huge difference in your future. The chemistry will fuel and deepen your relationship with yourself and fire up your ability to create lasting and significant relationships with others. In the workplace, your Chemistry Factor is an ace up your sleeve.

In the next chapter we will delve more deeply into values, the key elements behind authentic connection. Values are the secret power source of your Chemistry Factor.

THREE

VALUES CREATE CHEMISTRY

I was working as a recruiter with an unemployed CFO I had worked with in the past. He called me frequently to ask about any open positions I might have for him. When my answer was no he would become frustrated with me for what he perceived as a lack of effort on my part, as if I did not want to make a placement. Every time he called I dreaded the conversation before picking up the phone, knowing he would be pointing the finger at me for his being unable to find a job.

One day, due to a personal family matter, I had decided to empower the value of empathy. My wife's father, Sonny, was in the hospital in poor health, and sharing this value with my wife was helping her through this stressful time.

To empower empathy, I remembered a challenging moment in my life that had made a strong difference with my mother, Lois. She was on her death bed and I was holding her arm and shoulder with a supportive presence that made her passing one of caring and support. The next time the CFO called me I empowered the value of empathy within me and our conversation shifted. At the end of the call he thanked me for all my guidance and support. Later, after securing a new position through his own networking, he reciprocated the support back to me by passing on new job openings.

> *Your values become your destiny.*
> —Mahatma Gandhi

Your values are your rules of conduct. They characterize your sense of self and are elemental to the actions you take. They clarify your voice, focus your mind, and align your visions, allowing you to stay true to yourself. By knowing and being mindful of your values, you can match a value shared with another person. Values create the authentic-connection bridge to a great business relationship – the Chemistry-Factor connection.

Here is my definition of a value: It defines a belief you hold important, that you value. When you are empowered by a value it inspires your thoughts, encourages you to act with confidence, and sets the foundation for who you are at work and in the world.

Note that my definition of a value differs from what most people think it is. Societal values – often known as *ethics* – are generally shared uniformly. People agree, for example, that murder is wrong. The kind of values I'm talking about, however, are unique to each individual, therefore they can be a major source of unrealized friction in relationships. And a coworker's definition of a specific value can be decidedly different from yours.

There are two ways in which values can create stress and frustration at work. One revolves around the values that disconnect us from each other through either different definitions and/or different priorities. My value of honesty, and how I define it and its importance at work, might be different from yours. I might believe that a person is still an honest person even if they tell a white lie to protect another's feelings; there are some who would not agree with that.

Values can also create stress and frustration when there are unwelcome circumstances, projected disappointment, or thwarted expectations. When things are just not working out as planned it can be easy to get upset with either yourself or someone you work with. This upset is an alarm that tells you you're disconnected from a value you hold important – perhaps, for example, confidence. This disconnect can drain your energy and enthusiasm.

We all have countless values, but they are often condensed into all-encompassing ones. A core value such as integrity is made up of many root values that we often (incorrectly) perceive as one. When someone tells me a person lacks integrity, for example, I ask them to better define it. Did they disconnect from the value of dedication to excellence by settling for a weaker result; was the value of support for a fellow worker not met in accomplishing a task; or something else? The value of integrity can be a catchall for many values.

We all have values in common with everyone we work with. The Chemistry Factor Program has you explore which values you have in common with others and which you don't. Once you understand the distinction you can authentically connect with anyone using a value you have in common while still being true to yourself. Doing this increases your confidence and self-assurance, adding greater inspiration and energy to your work.

VALUES UNLOCK THE CHEMISTRY

We will be exploring a four-step process that guides your path to greater business relationships:

1. Name your values

2. Empower your values

3. Discover the values of others

4. Match values to ignite authentic connections with others

Some people you meet seem to have very different values from you, yet by using *value-matching* you can make a very positive and powerful connection with anyone.

CHEMISTRY-FACTOR VALUES

For some, the term *value* plays out as an ethical standard around what is right and what is wrong. But thinking that values are either right or wrong can limit your view of them. There is also lots of potential trouble when one person's ethical standard is used as a measure or judgment against another's.

The Chemistry Factor Program chooses not to weaponize values, but to use them as connectors. Chemistry-Factor values are used to create a positive connection by matching one of your values to a value you have in common with another person. This is a powerful way to use values. Connecting instead of judging is so much more productive in your relationships with your coworkers, and therefore so much more valuable to your greater business success!

Just as chemistry works with its elements, the Chemistry Factor works with its values – yours and those of the person with whom you are developing a relationship. When you find a value you share, and you choose to interact through that value, you find the alignment that creates your authentic connection. Person by person, interaction by interaction, you gradually learn to master your Chemistry Factor, which brings greater success to your relationships and business!

MISMATCHED VALUES

As unpleasant as it may be, we must take a moment to look at what happens when values are mismatched. Mismatched values lead to discord and stress, which then lead to disconnection, which makes the creation of powerful relationships essentially impossible.

MISMATCHED VALUES = DISCORD AND STRESS

Mismatched values are the most potent culprits in poor connections. Any difficult relationships you have with your coworkers can be traced back to mismatched values.

For many in business, stress, or the anger associated with it, is a motivator. Without it they will not get the job done well. It's what focuses them on their work. They use it as a formula for their success, and it works. There have been many highly successful executives throughout time who used stress not only to accomplish their work but to pressure others to do the same.

Jacob was a well-respected partner with an advertising agency in New York City. He was the type who consistently accomplished great strategic work, but always at the last minute. He identified himself as a procrastinator, and stress was what motivated him to get the work done.

At one point he began having issues with the people at work, developing a short fuse that could cause his temper to explode, negatively impacting everyone around him. He realized that by leaving so many things to the last minute he placed added pressure on himself to accomplish the work and allowed too many incompletions.

It's easy to fall into the trap of believing that the person you are communicating with is missing a value that you esteem. But remember that both you and the other person are always invoking a value in your interactions, whether consciously or not. The so-called "missing value" is actually a case of mismatched values. The key to getting to the chemistry of the situation is recognizing the mismatch and finding a value that both of you connect to. And this is exactly what the Chemistry Factor Program shows you how to do!

I have heard many words that describe a person's feeling toward their job and career when their workplace is congested with mismatched values... but I won't repeat the foul ones here. Two words I will repeat are *discord* and *stress*.

DISCORD

Your job becomes hard work when you are disconnected in your workplace, because without true connections with your coworkers there is discord.

For example, consider a situation in which you do not have a Chemistry-Factor relationship with your supervisor and he is micromanaging you. As a counterpoint to the micromanaging, your value of, say, independence gets revved up, and you find yourself in a tough work situation – one that does not serve you at all. If you continue to hold on to your value of independence, you feed the disconnect and your supervisor continues to distrust your ability.

In an example like this one, neither of you can get past the "insult" of the mismatched value, and neither of you feels valued. Before you know it you can become like two antlered bucks stuck in a headlock, with only discord fueling your work together. This is not good for the success of either of you.

STRESS

When you think of work, and the feeling that overwhelms you is stress, you know that the chemistry is missing. You know that you are not feeling authentically connected with the people you work with, and you are probably not feeling authentically connected with yourself. Drilling down deeper, you know you and your values are out of sync. This means that value-matching with anyone else is virtually impossible, and you get stressed. Unfortunately stress leads to more stress, a downward spiral is created, and you become a walking time bomb, like Jacob.

DISCORD AND STRESS = DISCONNECTION

If you haven't created values-based authentic connections with your coworkers, you are working in the land of discord and stress, creating disconnection. This leads to a yet greater chance for disconnected relationships with coworkers, offering fewer possibilities for authentic relationships and limiting your career success. You might be the person others try to avoid, either consciously or unconsciously.

DISCONNECTION WITHIN

Discord and stress manifest into all kinds of internal disconnection. Symptoms include:

- An uncertainty that makes you harshly question yourself
- A nagging feeling that you are not seen, heard, appreciated, or respected
- A stumbling reluctance to take action
- A less than optimistic view of your work and career

DISCONNECTION WITH OTHERS

If you don't look forward to running into coworkers in the office, or feel you are not part of the team at work, you are disconnected. There are numerous reasons you don't want to feel disconnected at work. They range from the fact that you likely spend more waking hours at your job than anywhere else to the realization that disconnection from your coworkers harms your long-term goals for career and business success.

THREE LEVELS OF DISCONNECTION

Without the strong relationships that come from matched values, there are three levels of disconnection:

1. **MIA connection:** With a missing-in-action connection, you are each living in what you think is missing and have staked out your own corner of the ring – upset, angry, and blaming the other person. You are focused on the value you think the other person is missing instead of how you can find a matching value. Neither you nor the other person is even trying to connect. Not only is there no connection, but there are big breakdowns in communication in general.

   If these are the kinds of relationships you have with your coworkers, you can imagine how even one of your MIA connections can change everything about your work day or long-term plans with the company. It is easy to imagine how it could affect and infect your company. The company's overall employee engagement, productivity, and bottom line can be thrown off kilter by toxic work relationships, and you could be blamed. This is not a good situation.

2. **Misconnection:** In misconnection situations, you are trying to connect, but it really does take two to tango; it's like trying to fit a square peg into a round hole. There is a line for communication, but it tends to be "down" on a regular basis, so communication is sporadic and authentic connection is not happening. On an individual level, both you and your coworker are left feeling

frustrated and burned out. These feelings seem to filter into the ventilation system and spread throughout the company. There is a reason your coworker is not connecting with you: they are already infected with the misconnection toxin.

3. **Low-level connection**: A low-level connection provides some connection, but it is hard work to get any chemistry flowing. There may be some overlap in the values that you are each filtering your interaction through. It's interesting that this level of connection is all many of us expect at work – *work* and *hard work* are synonymous, so the fact that connection is difficult is acceptable.

The cure for the discord and stress of disconnection is the value-matching that creates Chemistry-Factor relationships with your coworkers. Your Chemistry Factor is urgently needed.

VALUE–MATCHING
=
AUTHENTIC CONNECTION

At first take, value-matching might seem too simple to have a big impact. One could easily revert to an "I just need to work harder" or "I need to think of the next big idea to impress my colleagues" solution for growing their career, but do little to energize and inspire better relationships and greater success in the long run.

But you will keep reading because you get that having values-based connections at work creates prosperity for everyone, especially you. Further, you get that creating authentic connections and great business relationships easily and with a wide range of people is the Chemistry Factor you want! Who wouldn't?

INSTEAD OF DISCORD

Let's go back to the antler-lock story: we left you and your micromanaging supervisor locking horns...

One of my clients, Tracy, a client finance manager, was being micromanaged by her new client finance director. She was expected to explain every detail of her client-forecasting process, which had never been questioned by her previous director, who had left for a new opportunity. Every day she had to explain her reasoning for client-revenue recognition, expense analysis, labor-hour projections, etc. This took up a tremendous amount of time – double work as she saw it. It was especially frustrating when she would be left in limbo waiting for her reports to be reviewed by a very busy director, unable to continue until they were approved.

She was angry and felt she wasn't trusted by her boss. Her value of trust was automatically disconnecting her every time she worked with him. She dreaded working with him and was ready to leave the company.

I discussed with Tracy that the director was new and wanted to be sure the work that went out was correct. Her reply was that over the past three months there were at most a few minor changes in her work that made no difference to the budget or variance analysis. She felt that she had more than proved her abilities. Upon reviewing her values, she realized that her value of independence was the real culprit in her frustration; she did not like being second-guessed on every small detail.

Tracy's relationship with her boss was on autopilot disconnect caused by what she believed was a lack of trust.

39

In our coaching she learned to empower her value of trust, which helped her overcome her resistance to change.

When she switched gears and authentically connected to the value of trust with her director she began trusting him rather than giving him lip service to get through the ordeal of not being given the independence she wanted. In a short time she learned the director's methodology in doing the work and adapted it as her own. Her director soon became more comfortable with her work and she was given more and more independence to do it. She was amazed at the turnaround in their relationship!

Working from the common value of trust with her director supported his actions instead of making him wrong, which is what disconnection does. When someone is made wrong, they are more apt to want to prove themselves right with an "I'll show you" attitude. By authentically connecting to trust with her director, pressure was taken off him. Micromanaging is very time-consuming – one reason he was too busy to get all his work done. He was happy to now *trust* Tracy. One common value built a bridge in their relationship and other common values followed. Her opportunity for career advancement in the company went on the fast track with his support.

By using her Chemistry Factor, Tracy was able to authentically connect with her director through trust, and fire up their chemistry. In sections I and II of *The Chemistry Factor* you will learn how to identify your values, empower them, and create powerful, authentic connections just as Tracy did.

INSTEAD OF STRESS

Remember how Jacob was beginning to blow his top from the stress he created for himself by relying on it to motivate his actions? We discovered that he loved to snowboard – a great way for him to be in the moment, totally alive. He recalled how easy it was for him to fall down when he first started snowboarding. Each time he fell he would bounce back up again in order to get better. He felt sore at the end of the day, but it was his enthusiasm that got him back on the slopes the next morning.

His ability to connect to the value of enthusiasm at work by embracing his enthusiasm for snowboarding opened up a new perspective that not only lightened his load in meeting client deadlines but also made him much happier to be at the agency. He had used procrastination to create a sense of urgency to inspire his work, but procrastination had become counterproductive and self-sabotaging.

His enthusiasm motivated him because he wanted to improve his skills, and he did. Not only did his strategic skills become stronger, so did his people skills. He made work a game that allowed him to fall, get up, and get better – no more forced deadlines. He was on the "work slope" all day rather than at his desk energized to accomplish his work.

Imagine that because you have authentically connected values-based relationships with all the people in your company, you get up on Monday morning and look forward to going to work. Imagine that when discussing your workday with friends you find yourself speaking with animation and inspiration about all the great things that you and your coworkers are doing. Imagine that when offered a new opportunity with another company, you consider it, but must weigh it against a powerful list of pluses in your current position. Stress no longer makes you question your career direction. Now you'd rather emphasize its enjoyment. This picture looks great – and sounds amazing! Stop imagining and go get it!

WORKING WITH VALUES

You are beginning to see that having your values work for you rather than against you makes great sense. You're ready to create your Chemistry-Factor connections. Values rock!

But before moving on to the Chemistry Factor Program, there are a few things left to introduce you to:

YOUR VALUES VAULT

The more fully you explore your values the better. But because you want to balance the plethora of values with a focus that makes using them easy and efficient, I give you a Values Vault. It's a library of values, kept safe as gold bars are kept safe in a bank vault. And just as you would not want to be walking around with all your gold bars, you don't want to overwhelm yourself with all your values all at once. Yet you do need some "spending money," so this is not the kind of vault in which you lock away your treasures and never use them. Leave the door open! This is a vault because your values are important to you, but they are only valuable when you use them in your life and business.

The Size of Your Values Vault

Your Values Vault is on one hand endlessly expansive, but it's not a "bigger is better" proposition. You do not want to throw in every value you can think of just to fill your vault. If a value is not true to you, it doesn't belong in your Values Vault and will not carry any weight there.

Yes, the more values you have the more flexibility you have in matching values and creating chemistry. But a vault filled with false values has no value at all; it's an illusion. And if you build your greater success on an illusion, when that illusion eventually crumbles, your hard-won success might fade as well.

The good news is that there is a way to fill your Values Vault with your true values without compromising yourself. The Chemistry Factor has your back on this, too! (Chapters 4 and 5 show you how to do this.)

VALUES EVOLVE OVER TIME

At different stages of your life your values naturally shift. One of the best things about the Chemistry-Factor approach is that as a continuing practice it keeps you current on tuning in to your values and others' values. This means you are less likely to be working with a value structure that is outdated and feels awkward.

Most people spend little or no time consciously empowering their values, but in doing so you will decrease stress and improve your relationships. Just as you go to the gym or take up yoga to improve your health, staying consciously in touch with your values and empowering them produces greater benefits at work and in your life.

THE CHEMISTRY FACTOR PROGRAM SUMMARIZED

The style of your Chemistry Factor is unique to you, but the results of following the basic steps to create powerful business relationships with values-based authentic connections are the same for everyone: greater business success.

POWER UP YOUR VALUES

When your values are clear to you, it's easier to make decisions, take action, and live confidently. The first step in the Chemistry Factor Program is to name your values, and the second step is to empower them. You will discover the wealth of values you have at times felt in your gut but were unable to define. You will learn to lock them into habit so you can empower your values quickly and easily, connecting to them whenever you want to. These first two steps allow you to feel unlimited resonance with who you are. Connection to your values pays big dividends in your company and career because your values are both a foundation for you and a catalyst for matching values with others.

IGNITE AUTHENTIC CONNECTIONS

You will learn how to identify the values of others through Value-Discovery Conversations. This gives you insight into the coworker with whom you choose to connect. It also allows you to find a path along which you and the other person can stay true to yourselves and yet open to connection. You ignite the authentic connection by lighting up a value match. Making the value match is at the heart of the Chemistry-Factor process.

CREATE POWERFUL
BUSINESS RELATIONSHIPS

Once a value match is made and the authentic connection spark is lit, a "spontaneous combustion" leads to the creation of a powerful business relationship. As you master this chemistry you create a network of coworkers who work with and for you in positive and productive ways, and the power spreads far and wide, in your company and in your career. You are the "Paul" in your organization whose ability to authentically connect to his reactionary CEO made him his CEO's respected confidant! You have a potent Chemistry Factor!

HOW TO USE THE REST OF THIS BOOK

The Chemistry Factor is designed to heighten your Chemistry-Factor potential. In discovering the power of authentic connection, many people want to achieve it quickly. But skipping ahead or rushing to get to the next exercise will hinder your progress in enhancing your Chemistry Factor. Appreciate each exercise and practice strengthening their intended outcomes. You will reach your Chemistry-Factor proficiency faster if you go slow and steady.

THE CHEMISTRY FACTOR PROGRAM

I.

POWER UP YOUR VALUES

FOUR

NAME YOUR VALUES

You, and your values, are crucial parts of your Chemistry Factor. When you know *your* values, you know your *value.* The deeper and stronger your connection to your values, the more you have to work with when creating powerful business relationships. In this chapter we explore how you can dive in and really get to know yourself via the values you hold.

Quite honestly, if you did only this part of the Chemistry Factor Program you would be taking a big step toward your greater success. When you consciously know yourself at this core level and can connect with yourself, you naturally attract the success that enriches your life. But you will want to learn and use the entire Chemistry Factor Program to enjoy even greater benefits.

You will explore the range and depth of your values to strengthen your Chemistry Factor. You will begin by naming your values, then empowering them. I will take you step by step through the process.

THE IMPORTANCE OF NAMING YOUR VALUES

The act of naming is a powerful one. Naming gives a value status, and writing it down empowers it even more. If at first you have trouble naming your values, don't worry. Many people do. In my years of coaching executives I have found that when first asked, most people can only name a few of their values. A majority have trouble naming even three.

Once they begin to experience the benefits of understanding their values, this changes dramatically. They realize that they have many more values that are meaningful to them that they want to use.

If a CEO connects with their staff using only the value of dedication, they might be predictable, but will also be inflexible and boring. The more values a CEO uses to connect with their staff, the stronger their relationships and the more they inspire productivity and support.

I once worked for the president of a garment company who was always using the value of friendship with the people he worked with. People liked him, but they grew tired of his leadership, missing values such as commitment and decision-making. Friendship got in the way of his taking a stand. His staff lost confidence that he would deliver on the company vision.

After a year on the job he was asked to leave, having not met company goals. I know he had the values of commitment and decision-making; I saw him use them in his personal life. But his overwhelming value of friendship did not allow him to use them powerfully at work.

To support you in naming your values, there is a Chemistry Factor Values Reference List in appendix A at the back of this book. You can also go to www.thechemistryfactor. com/book to find a printable version of the list.

THREE LEVELS OF VALUE DISCOVERY

When you think about your Chemistry-Factor values, think in terms of three levels of discovery while noting that the levels are not meant to be hierarchical. All values are equally significant but they are discovered using different exercises in this chapter. Like peeling an onion, the exercises pertaining to each level provide different vantage points from which to uncover more of your values – some that may have gone unnoticed.

The three levels of Chemistry-Factor values are:

- Level 1: DNA Values (exercise 1)

- Level 2: Life-Story Values (exercises 2 and 3)

- Level 3: Discovered Values (exercises 5 and 6)

Level 1 is your DNA Values. These were passed on to you early in your life, often from parents and teachers. Many of your DNA Values come to you through your experiences as well. They are so important and so basic to you that they often work on autopilot in your life and work. A DNA Value of the president of the garment company in the story above was friendship.

In levels 2 and 3 you will use *value-mining* techniques to identify more values. The two types of mined values are Life-Story Values and Discovered Values.

For your level-2 Life-Story Values, stories are the mines you explore to research your value history. By reviewing your stories of challenge and success you will be able to extract your values. Stories reveal deeply ingrained values, making the insights garnered from them rich and profound.

Your level-3 Discovered Values are revealed through two different value-mining techniques. In the first you explore within yourself using an exploration exercise. In the second you identify your values through the people around you.

FILL YOUR VALUES VAULT

The "gold bars" you put in your Values Vault come from the values lists you create as you finish this chapter. Your Values Vault shows how often a value presented itself by level and frequency. (See appendix B or download it at www. thechemistryfactor.com/book.) Note that any value in your Values Vault is listed only once no matter how often it was repeated in your other lists. When you add a value to your Values Vault, increase by one the number in the column for the level it came from. Note the number of times it appears in each level. Use a pencil to keep track of the number of times it appears in each level and to change the number in the "Total" column. The more often it appears, the more powerful it likely is in your work and/or life. Your Values Vault is your go-to source for remembering the values you have discovered and can use in your work.

YOUR VALUES LISTS

There are two important things to remember about your values lists:

1. Duplication: It is very likely that some values will appear in all levels of your values lists. There will even be values that show up many times on the same list. Don't worry if this happens. In fact, if a value keeps appearing, it indicates that particular value is important to you. Pay attention to such duplications. This analysis helps you as we progress in this chapter to better understand the values you are prone to use in your relationships and those you are not.

2. Less than perfect: Don't try to figure out the "perfect" values lists. There is no such thing, and your values evolve and change over time. The goal of the Chemistry Factor is to create powerful business relationships, and that comes via authentic connection. The more expansive you are in creating your lists of values, the easier it will be to connect.

YOUR OWN NAMES FOR YOUR VALUES

The Chemistry Factor Program includes the Chemistry Factor Values Reference List (see appendix A) to help you name your values, but this doesn't mean you're restricted to the names on the list. I encourage you to name values that are not on the list. Sometimes an unusual name resonates with you. For example, you might name a value "chutzpah" instead of using the more traditional "audacity" or "courage." Don't hesitate to use names that have special meaning for you. They're yours and nobody else's. They make you unique.

PERSONAL VALUES = WORK/CAREER VALUES

Some people feel they must separate their personal values from their work/career values. This is like separating the icing from the cake. In fact, trying to separate them just complicates matters. It's best when your personal and work/ career values are congruent.

LEVEL 1: DNA VALUES

This list is your launching pad, giving you the first elements in strengthening your Chemistry Factor and providing a valuable resource.

The term *DNA Values* is an indication of how these values have been with you from the beginning. Some of them are inherited from your early experiences of success. Many you have picked up from the people around you: parents, teachers, friends, and mentors. In many cases you picked them up subconsciously.

To this day I find that my approach to work is grounded in a value of dedication that my parents taught me and my first job experience instilled in me. I took my first job at the age of ten as a newspaper delivery boy. Working a paper route that stretched about two miles up and down my neighborhood streets, I delivered seventy-five papers a day, seven days a week, through rain, snow, and heat. The job took me about an hour and a half each day – longer on collection days. The extra spending money was great, but the responsibility of delivering papers every day could be exhausting.

I realize that what kept me going for two years on this job was my attachment to dedication. I witnessed my father's dedication to his job and my mother's dedication to practicing as a classical concert pianist. Throughout my life I connected to this value quite spontaneously, as if on autopilot.

You, too, will find that many of your DNA Values are on autopilot. This is both good and bad. Once you have completed your DNA Values List, ask yourself when these values serve you and when they don't. When a DNA Value inspires your actions, it is serving you. But sometimes it does not serve you, and you might be unconsciously self-sabotaging yourself by holding on to it.

It's like an addiction. I can think of many instances in which connecting to dedication made work harder for myself and the people I worked with. When I worked at a CPA firm after college I was encouraged to work late – the greater the billing hours, the higher the fees for the firm. It was at times a game to see who would stay later. But the later I worked the less productive I was. Dedication led to overkill.

Anytime you find yourself reacting to a circumstance that is upsetting you, it is likely that you are the victim, not the master, of a disconnected DNA value. The value is controlling you; you are not controlling it.

DNA Values are likely to show up on all levels of your values lists. They were part of you early on and have been guiding lights throughout your life. Understanding how and when to use them is enlightening.

EXERCISE 1
CREATE YOUR LEVEL-1 DNA VALUES LIST

1. Review the Chemistry Factor Values Reference List. (See appendix A or download it at www. thechemistryfactor.com/book.)

2. Choose about ten or eleven values and write them down as your DNA Values List. (See appendix C or download it at www.thechemistryfactor. com/book.) Choosing DNA Values is more art than science. Choose the values you feel most connected to. That said, here are some tips for identifying your DNA Values:

   - "I feel great": When you think about a value, it feels great. You are on solid footing with this value, and it is powerful and comfortable.

   - The value feels clear and simple: The idea of the value rings true. You don't feel ambiguous about standing by this value.

   - The value has an impact on you: The value impacts you in a way that makes you feel stronger and more energized. It motivates and inspires you.

3. Add your DNA Values to your Values Vault, placing a "1" in the DNA Values column.

Please wait at least one day before moving on to exercise 2, and do no more than one exercise per day in chapter 4 to give them time to sink in.

LEVEL 2: LIFE-STORY VALUES

Because the richest mines are your stories, begin your value-mining here. The excavation process is designed to give you an interesting and insightful look at your life.

USE YOUR STORIES

Your life stories and other stories that inspire you are great places to mine for values. They are important resources because the stories you remember, and how you articulate them, tell you a lot about yourself. Look at two types of stories: Peak-Moment Success Stories and Challenging-Moment Stories.

As mentioned earlier, there is no reason to distinguish between your personal and work values. Therefore, in mining for values, there is no reason to limit yourself to only personal or only work stories. All of your stories reveal values that are important to you.

PEAK-MOMENT SUCCESS STORIES

I'm sure you have had many Peak-Moment Success Stories. You can use your own personal and business/career stories or stories from movies, books, or other media. The qualifying point is that the story inspires you. These are experiences that make you feel very happy or proud, or are particularly meaningful or memorable.

They do not have to be current stories. You might have a Peak-Moment Success Story from when you had your first job or your first promotion. It might be an event such as the first time you met your spouse. Recalling these stories is useful and rewarding on many levels, and they provide fertile ground for uncovering many of your values.

Here is one of my personal Peak-Moment Success Stories:

Home Run

I played on a little league baseball team named the Giants. We had the best record in the league and some of the best players. I was a first-year rookie. I wanted to succeed and I practiced my swing every day for hours, focusing on one spot on our backyard fence.

Midway through the season I was playing as a substitute. I went to the plate and everything came together in that moment: I could see the ball clearly, my swing felt strong, and I hit a line drive home run over the green monster in left field. With my dad and sister in the stands, I watched the ball sail out of sight. It was a moment I will remember for the rest of my life.

Rounding the bases was like floating on air. I got high fives from my manager, and good-natured ribbing from my teammates. I became a starting player and played full games for the rest of the season.

EXERCISE 2
VALUE-MINE YOUR
PEAK-MOMENT SUCCESS STORIES

Finding and extracting your values from your Peak-Moment Success Stories is a two-step process. First write your stories down, then identify and extract the values.

1. Write your stories

    a. Start with the first story that comes to mind. Write it down. Don't worry about punctuation or spelling. You know this story, so just write it down as if you were telling it to a friend. If you are more comfortable speaking the story, you can record it, then transcribe it. Write the whole story, and include as many specific details as you can remember. You might write a first draft, then revise it by adding details.

    b. Write down another story. Remember, these can be your own stories or cautionary stories from other sources. Whether a personal or career story, yours or someone else's, the key is that for whatever reason it creates a challenge within you.

2. Extract the values

    Once you have written down at least two stories, identify and extract the values from them, one story at a time. You will be taking notes, so you can use a hard copy of your story and take notes on a separate piece of paper or in the story itself (see the sample below this exercise), or use the comment feature in your writing software. Have the Chemistry Factor Values Reference List handy. (See appendix A or download it at www.thechemistryfactor.com/book.)

    a. Choose a story and read it once.

    b. On the next read, use the Chemistry Factor Values Reference List to help you identify values that you associate with specific passages of your story. Record the values you discover.

c. Continue to read and extract values until there are no more values to discover in the story. You should read it at least three times to extract all the possible values, and list them in your Life-Story Values List. (See appendix D or download it at www.thechemistryfactor. com/book.)

You will be surprised by how even the simplest of stories can reveal multiple values. In fact, in every sentence there are multiple values to be found. Extracting the values also reveals that your values are "at work" all the time. Being conscious of your use of your values is a smart Chemistry-Factor move, one that leads to greater success.

The value extraction for my Home Run story and another of my Peak-Moment Success Stories are on the following pages:

Home Run

action   *team play*

I played on a little league baseball team named the

fun   *success*

Giants. We had the best record in the league and some

challenge   *hunger to learn*

of the best players. I was a first-year rookie. I wanted to

hunger to succeed   *dedication to excellence*

succeed and I practiced my swing every day for hours,

focus   *determination*   *strategic thinking*   *vitality*   *proactive*

focusing on one spot on our backyard fence.

patience

Midway through the season I was playing as a

team play   *excitement*   *balance*

substitute. I went to the plate and everything came

experience   *focus*

together in that moment: I could see the ball clearly, my

aggressive

swing felt strong, and I hit a line drive home run over

encouragement

the green monster in left field. With my dad and sister in

joy

the stands, I watched the ball sail out of sight. It was a

big success

moment I will remember for the rest of my life.

completion   *accomplishment*

Rounding the bases was like floating on air. I got high

acknowledgment   *sense of humor*

fives from my manager and good-natured ribbing from

camaraderie

my teammates. I became a starting player and

leadership   *bonding*   *optimism*   *progress*   *contribution*

played full games for the rest of the season.

My Hong Kong Adventure

big-picture thinking   *commitment*
I had always dreamed of working overseas, and that
achievement   *problem-solver*
dream came true. I was hired as a CPA to audit a
challenge   *diplomacy*
partnership in Hong Kong. The partnership was between
the buying office of a giant clothing distributor and the
                          professionalism
U.S. manufacturing firm I was sent to represent. When
I landed at the airport a woman rushed up to me with an
encouragement   *connection*
embracing welcome. It turned out she thought I was
                    karma
someone else, but I felt it a sign that Hong Kong was
joy
glad I was there.

                   responsibility   *discovery*
At first I was there as an internal auditor to see how
the business was performing. There had been questions
         honesty   *open-minded*   *goal-oriented*
as to whether everything was being reported clearly.
I found that the person they had hired to keep the books
    organization
was incompetent and the parent company was not well
substance   *results*
organized financially.
    strategic thinking
After finding inconsistencies in the partnership, the
                    trust
firms broke the relationship, but I was asked to stay as
    reliability
the company's eyes and ears to protect their
              leadership
investments. I stayed there for seven years building a
entrepreneurial   *advancement*
successful 125-person buying office, was promoted to
dedication to excellence   *hunger to grow*
chief operating officer, and worked in seven different
                  enthusiasm
countries throughout Asia. It was a wonderful adventure
    accomplishment   *discovery*
– I learned a great deal, traveled extensively throughout
creativity   *networking*
the world, and built lifelong friendships, all while being
reward   *recognition*
handsomely rewarded.

CHALLENGING-MOMENT STORIES

It is not only our Peak-Moment Success Stories that carry insight for us; Challenging-Moment Stories are also ripe with values. Many even believe that both in general and in the context of Chemistry-Factor value-mining, our moments of challenge carry more import than our success stories.

Here is one of my Challenging-Moment Stories:

Double Cross

I was recruiting a senior position for a large advertising agency, working with the head of the department. I had sent her five or six candidates over the course of several months, and one was the obvious choice for the job.

Suddenly everything stopped, and a month went by without anything happening. In executive placement this is not unusual; jobs can change or be put on hold. In the course of waiting, the candidate accepted another opportunity with a competitor – again, not unusual.

I later discovered that the head of the department had sent my candidate to the competitor because she was leaving the company to work with that competitor. I was very angry that she went behind my back to introduce my candidate directly to her new agency in violation of our signed agreement. I could not prove what she had done because my evidence was from my candidate and it would have gotten him in trouble with his new firm, so I stayed quiet but steamed with resentment for being cheated out of a fee.

Finding and extracting your values from your Challenging-Moment Stories is a four-step process. As with your Peak-Moment Success Stories, you will write down your stories and extract the values. The difference with the Challenging-Moment Stories is that after extracting values from the story as is, you also reverse the challenging parts of your story and extract more values. In other words you revisualize the story's challenges as lessons, discover how empowering certain values could have changed the story dramatically, and change the story.

<u>**EXERCISE 3**</u>

**VALUE-MINE YOUR
CHALLENGING-MOMENT STORIES**

1. Write your stories

   These might be more difficult to write down, as they can bring up negative thoughts and feelings. Remember that there is a higher purpose in doing this, so dive in. Facing these stories has its rewards.

   a. Start with the first story that comes to mind. Write it down. Don't worry about punctuation or spelling. You know this story, so just write it down as if you were telling it to a friend. If you are more comfortable speaking the story, you can record it, then transcribe it. Write the whole story, and include as many specific details as you can remember. You might write a first draft, then revise it by adding details.

b. Write down another story. Remember, these can be your own stories or cautionary stories from other sources. Whether a personal or career story, yours or someone else's, the key is that for whatever reason it creates a challenge within you.

2. Extract the values

Once you have written down at least two stories, identify and extract the values from them, one story at a time. Use a hard copy of your story and take notes or use the comment feature in your writing software. Have the Chemistry Factor Values Reference List handy.

a. Choose a story and read it once.

b. On the next read, use the Chemistry Factor Values Reference List to help you identify values that you associate with specific passages of your story. Write down the values you discover.

c. Continue to read and extract values until there are no more values to discover in the story. You should read it at least three times to extract all the possible values, and list them in your Life-Story Values List. (See appendix D or download it at www.thechemistryfactor.com/book.)

3. Reverse the failure

A Challenging-Moment Story often centers on anger, frustration, and disagreement. In order to find Chemistry-Factor values, simply reverse the challenging aspects of the story. You will notice that the values ultimately extracted from a Challenging-Moment Story are ones you had not empowered or were disconnected from at the time of the story, which is what added the challenge to the situation.

a. Read the story again and go ahead and feel any emotions that come to you. Don't censor or judge yourself. Let yourself feel the challenging emotions.

b. Shift your perspective from seeing the story as a past or current challenge to seeing the story as a current *lesson.*

c. Imagine how the situation could have or can play out in a more positive way.

As an example, in my Challenging-Moment Story, a great benefit for me occurred with the candidate who attained the position, highlighting values. We built a long-term connection that brought me recruiting opportunities to fill as well as a trusting and supportive relationship. I also learned to have a stronger focus in my communications with clients and candidates, and the issue has never repeated itself.

4. Extract more values

Identify and extract the values that could have, and can currently change this story.

a. Read the story again.

b. On the next read, use the Chemistry Factor Values Reference List to identify values that would reverse the challenging aspects of the story. Write down the values you discover.

Continue to imagine values that would have changed, and will now change the story in positive ways. Read the story at least three or four times to extract all the possible values.

This exercise is rewarding on several levels. Moving your Challenging-Moment Stories into a more positive light is significant all on its own. You will additionally uncover the deeper values that challenges naturally evoke in you.

The reverse values I extracted from my Double Cross story are on the following page:

Double Cross

independence   *responsibility*
I was recruiting a senior position for a large
negotiation   *achievement*
advertising agency, working with the head of the
               skill
department. I had sent her five or six candidates over
support   *reward*   *contribution*
the course of several months, and one was the obvious
efficiency
choice for the job.

                   investment   *patience*
     Suddenly everything stopped, and a month went by
understanding
without anything happening. In executive placement this
strategic thinking   *acceptance*   *support*
is not unusual; jobs can change or be put on hold. In
action-oriented
the course of waiting, the candidate accepted another
                powerful communication   *leadership*
opportunity with a competitor – again, not unusual.
      strategic analysis
     I later discovered that the head of the department
        security   *trust*
had sent my candidate to the competitor because she
      powerful listening
was leaving the company to work with that competitor.
             honesty   *trust*
I was very angry that she went behind my back to
personal care   *problem-solver*
introduce my candidate directly to her new agency in
   balance   *challenge*
violation of our signed agreement. I could not prove
    fairness   *justice*   *full self-expression*
what she had done because my evidence was from my
proactive   *friendship*
candidate and it would have gotten him in trouble with
   well-being   *common sense*
his new firm, so I stayed quiet but steamed with
           effective
resentment for being cheated out of a fee.

EXERCISE 4
COMPILE A FULL LEVEL-2 LIFE-STORY VALUES LIST

1. Gather all the values lists you created while value-mining your Peak-Moment Success Stories and your Challenging-Moment Stories.

2. Create a full Life-Story Values List. (See appendix D or download it at www.thechemistryfactor. com/book.) You might find it helpful to alphabetize this list. If a value is already on your DNA Values List, don't worry about the duplication. You can list the values as many times as they came up, or with numbers beside them indicating the number of times they appeared, which you will note in your Values Vault.

3. Add your Life-Story Values to your Values Vault, enter the number of times they came up, and update the "Total" column.

LEVEL 3: DISCOVERED VALUES

In addition to using your stories as mines for value-mining, there are other value-mining techniques you can use to reveal your Discovered Values:

EXERCISE 5
VALUE-MINE YOUR DISCOVERED VALUES

1. Complete the sentence "I value..." ten times. Write quickly and without thinking about what you are writing. Review what you wrote. If any response is in terms of a goal, idea, memory, desire, etc., translate it into a value.

2. Complete the same sentence, "I value...", ten more times.

3. Compile your Discovered Values List from what you value-mined above. (See appendix E or download it at www.thechemistryfactor.com/book.)

Here is a list I blurted out in half a minute, then reviewed for interpretation:

I value:

Word	=	Value Interpretation
Love	=	Deep Connection
Clouds	=	Freedom
Friendship	=	Friendship
High Fives	=	Success
Reward	=	Acknowledgment
Calm	=	Calm
Confidence	=	Self-Confidence
Discovery	=	Adventure
Smiles	=	Sense of Humor
Success	=	Achievement

Notice that after some thought I interpreted the original blurts as identifiable values. Transforming an unconscious thought, once reflected upon, into an "I value" statement can open a door for you to discover another value or give deeper insight to the meaning of a value. "Clouds" above is a good example of this. The metaphor allows me to better experience the freedom.

EXERCISE 6
ASK OTHERS

1. Ask colleagues, at work and in your network, what values they see reflected in you. Write them down.

2. Ask friends and loved ones what values they think are important to you. Write them down.

3. Ask your teachers and mentors what values they notice in you. Write them down.

Not only is this exercise illuminating, but it can also get some great conversations going... and this can, of course, lead to better relationships. Win-Win!

EXERCISE 7
COMPILE A FULL LEVEL-3 DISCOVERED VALUES LIST

1. Gather all the values lists you created while value-mining in exercises 5 and 6.

2. Create a full Discovered Values List. (See Discovered Values List in appendix E or download it at www.thechemistryfactor.com/book.) Remember, it's okay if a value is already on a previous list. Alphabetize the list if you find that helpful.

3. Add your Discovered Values to your Values Vault, enter the number of times they came up, and update the "Total" column.

Your Values Vault has been filling up and is giving you a greater understanding of what makes you who you are. In the next chapter you will create a Power Values List and learn to empower your values.

FIVE

EMPOWER YOUR VALUES

When you are inspired by a value, you are empowering it and ready to act from its perspective. It's likely you now have many values to work with in your Values Vault. Thirty or more is a good start.

For them to be most useful to you, it is important to learn how to focus in on the values that really resonate. Otherwise the task becomes overwhelming; you'll be like a baseball manager trying to play everyone at the same time. Yes, you might have a deep bench, but at any given moment your job is to get the right value to the plate or on the field. For this reason, the first step in empowering your values is to select a set of *Power Values.*

YOUR POWER VALUES

Your Power Values are those that are important to you and relevant to your current situation, both professionally and personally. In chapter 4 you explored values by looking at your past and present. In this chapter you will choose your Power Values by examining your Values Vault to determine which ones will move you into a future you proactively define. These are values that are lined up with your current goals and challenges – the ones you want front and center in your work right now.

First you will explore some of your goals and challenges at work. By focusing on what you want to achieve you will identify the values to help get you there.

For these exercises, a *goal* is a specific achievement toward which effort is directed; for example: win a new million-dollar client. The values that could help you achieve this goal might be dedication, excellence, and competitiveness. A *challenge* is a difficulty in an undertaking or relationship that you are stimulated to improve; for example: you're not getting along with your supervisor and want to create a more supportive two-way dialogue. The values that could help you overcome this challenge might be listening, commitment, and curiosity.

EXERCISE 8
IDENTIFY POTENTIAL POWER VALUES

Use the Goals and Challenges Worksheet (See appendix F or download it at www.thechemistryfactor.com/book.)

1. List two or three of your most important goals for the next year. (You can start with just one goal if you prefer.) Give this some time and play big with the goals you want to achieve. When you envision reaching a goal it should inspire you.

2. Using your Values Vault, identify three to five values you feel will best inspire you to accomplish each goal. Don't worry about repetition. It is perfectly okay if you repeat a value with a different goal.

3. Enter at least one goal from steps 1 and 2 with its values on the Goals and Challenges Worksheet.

4. List two or three important challenges you will face in the next year. Again, give it some time and think major inspirational transformation.

5. Use your Values Vault as a reference to identify three to five values to help you deal with each challenge. Again, repetition is perfectly okay.

6. Enter at least one challenge from steps 4 and 5 with its values on the Goals and Challenges Worksheet. Make note of how many times each value shows up in your Values Vault and at what

level(s). How prevalent has this value been in your work?

This exercise should provide you with a list of potential Power Values to choose from that you will then empower. To empower a value is to genuinely connect to it in a way that inspires your thoughts and actions in achieving your goals quickly and successfully.

EXERCISE 9
CHOOSE YOUR POWER VALUES

You are now ready to begin choosing up to eleven Power Values. For this exercise, go to Appendix G or download the Power Values List at www.thechemistryfactor.com/book.

1. Test the potential Power Values you chose in exercise 8 by envisioning each one as a catalyst for achieving your goals or transforming your challenges. To take on the goal or challenge, does the value feel:

   - Powerful and comfortable?
   - Clear and simple?
   - Energizing and motivating?

2. Choose the values that fit most powerfully with achieving your goals and transforming your challenges. Add these to your Power Values List. Limit the number of DNA Values on your Power Values List. For each DNA Value choose one that is

not. It's time to expand the values you use at work beyond those in your DNA. Trying to create the perfect Power Values List is counterproductive; enjoy the process and know that any value that reached this point is a powerful one.

3. Over time you will confirm eleven Power Values – no more at the start, as more than that can be overwhelming. If you are struggling to get to eleven, no worries. Choose three and move on to the next exercise. More will follow when you're ready.

EMPOWER YOUR VALUES

While your Power Values List will always be evolving and growing, for now you have no more than eleven. It's time to consciously empower your Power Values (exercises 10 through 15) so your connection to them is deep and they are ready to use for authentically connecting with others.

The first step in empowering your values is to authentically connect with yourself! With practice, any value you want for a Chemistry-Factor connection can instantly be empowered whenever you choose. In general, the more powerfully you empower a value, the more valuable it is to you in creating powerful business relationships for greater success.

EXERCISE 10
CHOOSE A POWER VALUE

1. Read the values on your Power Values List.

2. We humans can complicate even easy instructions, so pick an "easy" value to work on first.

Don't pick the one that's the most "you." In other words, don't try to pick the most impressive value; just pick one that feels good, one that is calling you, one that brings a smile to your face. Eventually you will empower all eleven values on your Power Values List, so there's no reason to put much weight on which value to start with.

EXERCISE 11
FOCUS AND CLEAR

To empower a consciously chosen value, you want an open mind and a clear head, otherwise you can unconsciously resist empowerment of the value. Without clarity, your old habits and fears can make choices that don't empower you.

1. You have five physical senses: sight, smell, touch, hearing, and taste. Pick the sense that's easiest to focus on. I'm very attuned to sight, so I used sight in the examples below.

2. Focus on something nearby and look at it as carefully as you can. For example, my desk chair is made of wood and fabric. The wood is brown with varnish streaks of various shades, and it's upholstered in brown and reddish fabric that looks like the dots in a pointillist painting. The seat is indented from my sitting on it, and there are wear lines and creases across the backrest. Go deep into what you see.

3. Within seconds this simple observation took me into a focused moment and allowed me to clear my head of every other thought. Use this clear space to consciously focus in on the value you chose in exercise 10.

Another way to focus and clear is to focus on your breathing, feeling the air go in through your nose and out of your mouth, over your lips. Do this with several breaths, clearing your thoughts, being mindful of the present.

"Focus and Clear" can be used to prepare for many of the exercises in this book. Focusing helps you open your mind for any task or exercise. If you find yourself out of focus, just repeat the exercise.

EXERCISE 12
UNDERSTAND THE VALUE DEEPLY

1. Write down the name of your chosen value at the top of a sheet of paper or computer document.

2. Immediately write down any thoughts, feelings, or stories about the value that come up. Take just three to five minutes to do this. Don't worry about spelling, punctuation, or structure; this helps you overcome blocks of apathy or self-criticism. It's not to get it "right," but rather to allow deeper access to what will empower the value. If it's more comfortable for you to speak, record it and transcribe what you said.

3. Read what you wrote and respond to it by diving into a deeper examination of the thoughts, feelings, or stories evoked in step 2.

4. Write your definition of this value. Keep it simple, from a few words to a sentence. This is not about getting it "right"; it's your unique definition of this value.

5. Write down the ways you think this value can serve you in the future.

EXERCISE 13
LOCATE THE VALUE IN YOUR LIFE

1. On the same sheet of paper or document that you started above, write down instances in which this value motivated or inspired you. (You might find that some of these were already expressed in exercise 2.) These can be from peak moments – yours or someone else's; a book or movie scene; etc. Choose instances that powerfully highlight this value for you.

2. Envision how the value will shine from you as you move through the world. Write down how it inspires achieving goals or transforming challenges.

3. Imagine a situation in which someone is talking about you and your success in terms of this value. Write down a description of this situation, including what the person said.

4. Notice how your body feels when you embrace this value. Are you relaxed or energized? How does your new connection to this value affect your physical being, from your head down to your toes? Write down what you notice.

EXERCISE 14
EMPOWER THE VALUE

Now that you have internalized the value, you understand it on a deeper level and can see where it is important in your life. From here, empowering the value is quite simple. It's like a conscious flick of a switch, and just as a light turns on instantly, so can your value.

Flick the switch, by visualizing the scenario from the sheet you completed in exercise 13 that best highlights this value, to make it light up within you. Bring your body to the feelings you wrote in step 4 of exercise 13 to making flicking the switch quick and easy. Feel the empowerment within you and let your thoughts and actions be guided by the perspective it gives you.

EXERCISE 15
EMPOWER ALL YOUR POWER VALUES

This is a process you shouldn't rush because going too fast can feel overwhelming. Empower another value, beginning again with exercise 10, and get it into your bones before moving to the next. Empowering one value can take a day or more. Empower it several times a day for as many days as it takes for your body to memorize it. It should be easy to consciously empower it when you want to. As you practice, the process becomes easier with additional values. When you feel comfortable with a Power Value, take on the next one. Everyone has a different clock for doing this. This is a great example of "The slower you go the faster you'll get there."

Put a checkmark in the "Power Values" column of your Values Vault to indicate each value you empower.

As your Power Values become easier to connect to, you will have them ready to go and your Chemistry Factor will be ready for action.

CONNECT TO YOUR POWER VALUES

EMPOWER VERSUS CONNECT

Now that you know how to empower your values, you are ready to connect to them whenever you choose to. Empowering your values gives you the tools to quickly connect to them whenever you want to. When you are empowering a value, you are connected to it.

CONNECT TO YOURSELF

In later chapters, you will learn how to use your empowered Chemistry-Factor values to authentically connect with others. The focus now is to use your Power Values to authentically connect with yourself.

When a challenging situation comes up, and as you go about your life and work every day, your Power Values are there to support you. They help you take action to make decisions and choices that deeply align with who you truly are. When you are connected to a Power Value by flicking the switch (exercise 14), you can then use the Power Value as a filter on how you perceive any given situation. This filter is invaluable, making your actions seem effortless!

One of my coaching clients was very frustrated with himself concerning a social media project he was strategizing for a Fortune 500 company. The ideas he offered to the client were shot down as either too complicated or not innovative enough. His clients came to think of him as an A strategist providing C work.

My client, Michael, felt tired and stressed; the longer he worked, not meeting expectations, the harder the work got. He was a strategic thinker experiencing what you might call a strategic block. When we talked it was clear that the pressure of delivering a winning plan that met expectations while flying solo had his creative juices going in too many directions with no finish line in sight. He felt lost without a rudder.

Michael had combined the many social media strategies that had always worked in the past, using the same DNA-Value success formula he had always used. But now he was being asked to develop a different strategy. So he decided to look at his situation from a new value perspective, one that he had never used for creating a social media plan.

Michael was skilled at developing and guiding project management using his strategic plans, and clients insisted on his doing so. To accomplish this he relied on two values for success: discipline and collaboration. But he had never used discipline or collaboration to create a strategic plan for social media; these values seemed antithetical to the strategic thought he was trying to inspire. Yet he gave it a try.

Through the lens of discipline, he created a foundation and timeframe that better organized his use of time. He was a free thinker when it came to strategy, which made it more difficult for him to stay on task. Discipline kept him on the task at hand, staying with each milestone until completion. When he empowered collaboration, he discovered that his coworkers added ideas and perspectives that had not occurred to him. He was inspired by their innovative thinking, opening a well of new ideas that led to a successful plan that expanded the client's customer base at minimal cost.

EXERCISE 16
CONNECT TO A POWER VALUE

1. Consciously recognize the disconnect of a current challenging situation. When you're disconnected from yourself, you feel upset, frustrated, angry, fearful, and/or bored. Pay attention to these signals.

   When you can't realize you are disconnected from yourself and your values, you tend to get stuck in the disconnection without even realizing there's a problem – which is a big problem, one that limits your success.

   I've known many executives who had a chip on their shoulder because they did not feel appreciated. This becomes a disconnect that has a negative effect on their work and the work of those around them. They are stuck in a disconnected value – appreciation – that does not serve their success, and they have become numb to it. They don't realize they can simply connect to a value such as collaboration to inspire their work again.

2. The good news is that when you are not connected with yourself, connecting through the filter of one of your values sets things right again. Follow these steps to connect:

   a. Consider the current situation you thought about in step 1, and choose a value from your Power Values List or from your Values Vault that you believe will have a positive impact on your disconnected situation.

   b. If you have not empowered the value, take it through the steps in exercises 10 through 14, including it as a new Power Value.

   c. Bring your attention to this Power Value and look at your current situation through the filter of this value. Take particular note of how this makes you feel about the situation.

   d. When you feel positive about how the value relates to the situation, connect to the value by moving forward from the perspective of that value.

As you create a stronger connection to a Power Value, new stories will be uncovered, allowing you to take that value connection to an even deeper level.

CONNECTION TRIGGERS
FOR YOUR VALUES

Once you have empowered and connected to a value, creating a connection trigger for it makes it even easier to access when you want to use it. The trigger can be a physical gesture or, if you want a subtler trigger, a thought, an image, a song, a sound, etc. The important thing is that the trigger evokes the feeling and energy of the value, not just a mental thought about it. It should evoke not just a definition of the value, but also the way you feel when the value is in play in your life.

Examples of physical gestures include snapping your fingers, making a fist, or simply taking a deep breath. For the value of organization, I interlock my fingers as if in prayer, triggering a feeling that everything is in its right place.

Feel free to use any of your five senses for a trigger. An example of using sound is a song trigger. The Queen song "We Will Rock You" was played by several of the sports teams I was on. It triggers my value of collaboration and team spirit.

A trigger can even be something that has no association with the value except that you are making one. For instance, for the value of collaboration your trigger could be the image of a majestic mountain. No one else need understand the connection as long as the image of the mountain triggers collaboration for you.

EXERCISE 17
CREATE A CONNECTION TRIGGER

The more vivid and clear your state of mind as you create the trigger, the better.

1. Choose one of your Power Values.

2. Connect to the Power Value.

3. Let the value find its trigger.

   a. Relax and let the best trigger for this value come to you. Trust what comes to mind.

   b. Once you have chosen a trigger, test it by asking yourself "Does it feel grounded and solid? Does it feel clear and simple?" The simpler it is, the stronger the connection. When it feels simple and solid, move to step four.

4. Lock in this trigger for this value simply by making the association repeatedly whenever you think about it over the next day or so.

The trigger now makes it easier for you to connect to and use your Power Value. Create one trigger at a time. Cement one in before creating another one. Add them to your Power Values List.

AN EXAMPLE OF THE STEPS TO EMPOWER AND CONNECT TO A VALUE

MY VALUE OF CALM

Step 1 (exercise 12)

Understand – free write

At peace with the world and moment, see everything in slow motion, in the zone, no upset, see moment, act from big picture, power to calm others. Ease of movement on the tennis court, playing football, fielding a baseball, hitting a baseball, at peace and love with family and friends. Embrace love, honeymoon in Greece with Tracey, moment with Aaron as little child on bed in NH vacation, on boat in St. Lucia, Joelle in car rhyming, big hug, sense of humor, joy and happiness, in the moment yoga, seeing the tennis ball hit the sweet spot, hugs with Tracey, bro, sis, mom, pop, beautiful sunset, the warm rain, flowers blooming, smell of the grass, peace of snow falling on the ski slope, embracing the moment and appreciating it for its unique beauty, relaxing on the beach with eyes closed, soft sun, listening to the waves, smelling and tasting the sea salt in the air, cooking, Siddhartha...

Definition

At peace and comfortable inside me with a great sense of connection and sharing

Serve me

In focus, appreciation for life, not about future or past, no expectation in the moment

Step 2 (exercise 13)

Locate a value-empowering peak moment

On the ski slope, top of the mountain, total whiteout, can't see my hand in front of me, standing stationary on my skis, no wind, heightened sense of silence, calm, easy breathing, and at total peace in the moment

Body sensations

Head, neck, and shoulders at ease, soft smile, body loose, voice drops an octave, life slows down while at the same pace, senses heightened, deep breathing

Step 3 (exercise 14)

Empower the value

Flick the switch; go to ski-slope moment, remember my body feelings

Step 4 (exercise 17)

Connection trigger

Right fist to left palm, Namaste, Buddha calm

IF WANTED, SHIFT VALUES

You will find that being connected to a Power Value can cover a lot of ground toward success. But situations come up when you want another value to help you through, so you can shift to a different value. The Chemistry Factor is successful because it gives you room for unlimited flexibility.

Having spent years writing this book, there were times I became very frustrated, thinking I would never finish it. I would be disconnected from my value of confidence. But when in this mindset there are many Power Values I can connect to.

I faced writer's block when I wanted to give you a storied example of value-shifting. Then I reconnected to my value of confidence, which brought me to share this story. I was writing in the now, connected to confidence, and no longer frustrated, but rather motivated. I value-shifted to optimism, which put a smile on my face, inspiring me to know that I will reach my goal of finishing this story, this chapter, and the book. There are moments when I'm writing when there are other Power Values I shift to in order to share the power of the Chemistry Factor. In this case, confidence and then optimism overcame my writer's block.

Note that when shifting values it's best to have only one value "up to bat" at any given time. Multiple values at the same time can get confusing, so if you bring in a new value, bench the one you were using.

EXERCISE 18
SHIFT VALUES

1. When the value you are working with isn't helping, choose a different Power Value OR a value from your Values Vault. All your Values-Vault values are ready because they've been vetted; you can empower one off the bench and put it into play. Ideally take it through the full empowerment process. Don't worry – the more practiced you are at empowering your values, the more quickly you can do this.

2. Connect to the new empowered value. (See exercise 16.) If you have created a connection trigger for the value, use it to make the connection. (See exercise 17.) Let the first value go and commit to the new value perspective.

Shifting values is not always easy. Sometimes it takes an extra effort to release the first value. Clearing your head helps you let go. (See exercise 11.)

Sometimes the value you're shifting to doesn't "take." One time I was suffering from a cold at work. Though I started out working from my value of commitment, it was not authentic; the physical interruptions of a stuffy nose and sore throat would not allow me to stay focused. I tried shifting to the value of confidence but that also wasn't helping me get my work done. I was working on a candidate search for an important client who wanted to fill a certified project director position quickly. I continued to stop and go in my search, forcing myself to be motivated but getting frustrated. And my frustration came across in my conversations with potential candidates. Confidence felt disingenuous every time I felt the pain of sneezing and my runny nose. Trying to shift to confidence while also being connected to commitment gave me a headache; I was faking it. So I focused, cleared my head by looking deeply into a statue of Buddha that sits on my desk (see Exercise 11), and decided to connect to the value of empathy, which I was not giving myself. Connecting to empathy for myself had me make the wise decision to go home and work from there. I took a hot shower, which opened my nasal passages. Feeling more comfortable, I found two potential candidates who agreed to be interviewed later that week. I normally would have chosen to tough it out instead, and I smile every time I think of that value shift. Now I use it not only for myself on occasion, but for others as well.

Shift values until you find one that truly connects with you and the given situation. Don't settle; the great thing about having all of these values to connect to is that there is always one that's a game-changer. Go for it.

RAISE YOUR CHEMISTRY-FACTOR GAME

EMPOWER MORE VALUES

It makes sense that the more values you empower, the more values you have ready "on deck," and the more powerful your Chemistry Factor. Feel free to choose and empower more values from your Values Vault and be ready to go.

UPDATE YOUR VALUES

Over time, monthly or bimonthly, update some of your values from your Power Values List and all three levels of your Values Vault to connect with them on ever-deeper levels. Updating allows you to apply them to additional goals and challenges while you continue to mine newly discovered values.

PRACTICE, PRACTICE, PRACTICE

To make sure your Chemistry-Factor connection to your values is cemented into place, be prepared to practice. Remember your peak moments, Power Values, and triggers. It can take time to cement them. To make it easier, do this one value at a time. When you lock one Power Value into place, add another and another until you have all of them memorized, as you did your multiplication tables in school. However, don't pressure yourself. When you're connected to a value it's enjoyable!

Even if you're only practicing, you will see results immediately. Meanwhile, others will notice that instead of upset, frustration, fear, anger, and/or boredom, you are reflecting all kinds of empowering and inspiring values.

In part I we've covered just the first two steps in the Chemistry Factor Program that are the catalyst for creating the authentic connections that lead to powerful business relationships.

OWN YOUR VALUES

You have created strong connections between yourself and your values. Don't discount these relationships. When you and your values are getting along, you are empowered in a big way. And as mentioned at the beginning of chapter 4, this part of the Chemistry Factor alone boosts your success.

One of the greatest benefits of getting to know your values is that your "value sensitivity" expands. You naturally pick up on more and more values that the people you work with connect to.

Just as an Alaskan can easily identify fifty types of snow while I can only identify the three I have shoveled (dry, wet, and icy), you are able to easily identify many more values in others. This is the key to building powerful business relationships.

THE CHEMISTRY FACTOR PROGRAM

II.

IGNITE AUTHENTIC CONNECTIONS

SIX

DISCOVER THE VALUES
OF OTHERS

It is now time to put on your Indiana Jones hat. You are about to become an explorer and archaeologist. There is a difference between you and Indiana Jones though: Instead of seeking valuable treasures, you are seeking the treasure of values. Specifically, you will be "digging" to discover the values of others. You will unearth the values they have consciously or unconsciously empowered in themselves.

You already have a vault full of treasures – your Chemistry-Factor values. Knowing your values is the first step in creating the kind of chemistry in your business relationships that leads to greater success. Envision now, however, knowing your values *and* being able to name the values of others. This provides you with both sides of the value-matching formula for creating the powerful chemistry that sparks authentic connection with another.

Many of you are informally value-matching with others already. It is natural to notice similar-minded people and connect with them. And, of course, in our personal lives we choose to spend most of our time associating with like-minded people. For instance, if you have strong political viewpoints, you likely spend a lot of your time with people who have the same basic political ideas. Of course this principle also works the other way. You can find yourself in conflict with people whose values are different from yours. This can be very limiting.

At work, you have less choice in who you associate and/or spend time with. You cross paths with all your coworkers whether or not there is an easy and clear path to authentic connection with them. But you have values in common with everyone at work. It is for you to discover them in order to authentically connect. The more different kinds of people you can easily and deeply connect with, the stronger your ability to create powerful chemistry in your business relationships.

To increase your success in value-matching, you not only want to fill up your Values Vault, you also want to be able to identify the values of the people you work with. In other words, being able to find value matches with as many people as possible is assisted by the depth and number of values you have identified within yourself.

Now that you have begun naming and empowering your values, you can interact more powerfully with others at work through your values. Notice how values lie at the heart of what people do and say. You are now consciously curious about what values prompt people's decisions and actions.

This chapter shows you how to excavate the values of the people at work. While it's not a common conversation to simply ask someone what their values are, you can be proactive in identifying them. Learning to elevate normal conversation to a Value-Discovery Conversation is a key Chemistry-Factor skill. We will look at both the mindset that makes this conversation easy to have and the steps that propel your excavation discoveries.

Because most of your value excavation will be done indirectly, it is a given that naming another person's values can be considered a guess – but it will be a well-informed Chemistry-Factor guess.

As you become more proficient in naming the values that people reveal, it is very possible that you will attain a deeper understanding of the values that drive these people than they themselves have.

THE VALUE-DISCOVERY CONVERSATION

Conversation is the basic communication tool in relationships of all kinds. Our conversations are both simple and complex, much like a simple movement of your arm is actually a series of complex muscle events orchestrated by a whole sequence of activities in your brain. A conversation appears as simply two people exchanging information, usually focused on the verbal part of the interaction. But there is other information communicated during a conversation that is often ignored or heard subliminally.

Listening powerfully for these other messages creates a "listener's mindset" that facilitates authentic connection.

In a Value-Discovery Conversation, your focus is on the listening aspect of the conversation. Remember, the more values you discover in this person, the better your chance of finding values you can match. This leads to Chemistry-Factor success, so it's important.

At first you will have to be conscious of the value-discovery aspect you add to your conversations, but eventually it becomes familiar and natural. You can have a formal Value-Discovery Conversation: You might meet with a coworker with the specific intention of exploring what values this person brings to their work. You might not ask them to name their values per se, but rather ask them what motivates their approach to a project. Such a question will unearth some of their values.

As you improve your value-discovery skills, these conversations become everyday conversations. It becomes second nature to continually expand your authentic-connection opportunities and strengthen your relationships.

A Value-Discovery Conversation looks very similar to a "regular" conversation from the outside, but it's also like an archaeological dig where you are looking not only for the information exchange but also for the "treasures" of that person's values. You will use both the right mindset and your Chemistry-Factor "digging tools."

SET THE STAGE FOR YOUR VALUE-DISCOVERY CONVERSATION

THE FIELD-TRIP MINDSET

In everything you do, your mindset matters. The right mindset essentially helps you get out of the way of your own thoughts and actions, and is therefore crucially important as you approach your Value-Discovery Conversations. I suggest the *field-trip mindset.*

Think back to your school days. You usually knew the basic what, who, where, and when of your day. On most days school was about passing the test, meeting expectations, and being judged. This default perspective is what I call the "test mentality." Most of us picked up this perspective from our early schooling and brought it to our adult work lives.

But there were also the field-trip days. Those days were special. You were taken to a new place for a new experience and it was exciting. Field trips brought out your sense of openness and curiosity. Field-trip days rocked no matter where you went or what you did.

This same perspective of discovery serves you in your Value-Discovery Conversations. The field-trip mindset is one of exploration and adventure – a receptiveness to new experiences and ideas, giving you a sense of enthusiasm. On some level you can feel like Indiana Jones.

Field-trip days had a completely different feeling from test days. You do not want your Value-Discovery Conversation to have the feeling of a test day. Instead you want that field-trip mentality of openness and curiosity as you search for a person's values.

OPENNESS

There was something special about the field-trip bus ride. No matter what else was happening in your class that week, that bus ride seemed to wipe the slate clean. It was as if you were given a fresh, blank canvas to paint on.

Since many of your work/career relationships are already established, openness is critically important as you ignite the chemistry in your current relationships. Established relationships have well-worn grooves to them. You have set up a working relationship with someone based on what you think of each other, but before you begin your Value-Discovery Conversation, you wipe that canvas clean. Starting over allows you to approach the discovery process in a fresh way, and this time you will not let various assumptions and unconscious values pile up. Instead you will set yourself up for a consciously open approach.

This does not mean throwing out what you already know. The field-trip mindset is about taking what you know and revising it or looking at it in a new light. It is about throwing what you know up in the air to see if it lands differently.

When you approach someone with field-trip openness, there is a much greater possibility that you will discover that they honor values you would not have thought of previously. For example, when I first started working for an executive recruiting company, I had a colleague, Sandra, from whom I felt very disconnected. I realized that the disconnection between us came from my lack of openness. In a misguided strategy, the owner of the company had stirred a pot of competition by telling me that Sandra wanted my clients and resented my success. He also told me that she lied. Naturally this put me on the alert.

When I bought the company, I realized that Sandra's success would be my success, and that our current relationship was draining and hurting us both. I decided to start over with a blank canvas and opened up to her by connecting to the value of honesty.

Well, it turned out that we had both been very guarded in our conversations, and the value of honesty connected us immediately. It was a breath of fresh air. We had many values in common and built an authentically connected relationship that served us both with greater success. We began splitting fees on some of the largest executive placements ever made by the company. When Sandra left the company, we continued to send each other holiday cards and stay in touch over the phone, and we still do ten years later.

The blank-canvas approach is a natural when you meet new people. But in your haste to fill the canvas, which is a natural human tendency, you might unconsciously use erroneous and limited judgments as your paintbrushes. So be thoughtful and generous in filling it. Better to let it fill in slowly, but with more potential for success. With new people, enjoy the blank canvas!

CURIOSITY

Albert Einstein said of himself, "I have no special talent. I am only passionately curious." And Walt Whitman advised, "Be curious, not judgmental." Both men give good counsel for the Chemistry Factor.

A thesaurus provides these two synonyms for the word *interest*: *curious* and *inquisitive*. On a practical level, this means you can show interest by listening closely and asking questions that allow your coworker to speak on a deeper level. Curiosity is part of the field-trip mindset because our childhood field trips taught us to be curious and our curiosity is what made the field trips so special. Curiosity will now help you excavate the values of others during your Value-Discovery Conversations.

EXERCISE 19
SET YOUR FIELD-TRIP MINDSET

This exercise focuses on a Value-Discovery Conversation with a coworker you already have a relationship with, so the first step is to get to the openness of the fresh, clean canvas.

1. Create openness.

   a. Think about the coworker you will be having your conversation with. Start easy with someone you already have a good relationship with and work with the goal of making it even better. (As you become more proficient you will advance to more challenging relationships.) Write the person's name at the top of a sheet of paper, or type it in a computer document, and list the values that you believe they consciously or unconsciously connect to. You can also add brief notes about why you believe these are the values this person honors. Use your Chemistry Factor Values Reference List, your Values Vault, and your Power Values List as references.

   b. Write or type the person's name at the top of a new page or document. This is your fresh, clean canvas. In step (a) you acknowledged that you know this person and can make educated guesses about their values. By starting a new page you are opening up to the idea that now, as a Chemistry-Factor archaeologist, you will be exploring and discovering new values or, at the very least, deeper aspects of the values you associate with that person. This turning the page to a blank one may seem too simple to have much effect, but you'll be surprised by how powerful this simple gesture can be.

c. Take this blank canvas to your Value-Discovery Conversation, whether metaphorically by just being open to what new discoveries you can make, or by actually taking it to your meeting, or, if meeting by phone, having it in front of you during the conversation.

The important part of this is to take the "energy" of steps (a) and (b) to your conversation.

2. Activate curiosity.

a. You also want to activate your curiosity about the person from whom you are going to extract values. To get into a curiosity-based mindset, think about what you already know about this person. You can take written notes or do this in your head.

b. From what you know, think about questions this knowledge evokes. For instance, if you noted that the person is really gifted in sales, you might want to know how they developed this skill. Write down open-ended questions – ones that cannot be answered with a yes or a no – that explore this curiosity. (Open-ended questions are explored a bit further below.)

c. Write down what you *don't* know about this coworker and think about what new information you would like to know. Write down open-ended questions that explore what you don't know. These questions are not specifically ones you will use in your Value-Discovery Conversation; you might ask some of them, but their real value is in instigating your curiosity about this person. Enjoy the questions themselves.

3. Enjoy your field-trip mindset.

The key to being open and curious is to *enjoy* yourself. As adults, especially ones in work situations, many of us lose our openness and curiosity and label them as childlike. The Chemistry Factor is bringing openness and curiosity back to you, and they will become important tools for your Chemistry-Factor success.

VALUES EXCAVATION

Once you have your field-trip mindset in place, you are ready to start excavating values. Before we move forward, a note about the word *excavate*. Yes, it fits with the Indiana Jones idea because he was an archaeologist. An archaeologist digs in and sifts through a landscape looking for artifacts that reveal things about the civilization that once inhabited that site. Excavation is the careful unearthing of these buried treasures.

In a similar way, you will be using your conversation skills to "dig up" values. By listening carefully and interpreting what you hear, feel, and see, you will discover some of the values of your coworker. These values are treasures because they are the essential elements for the chemistry of authentic connection.

Values are essential to everyone. You must take care as you seek to unearth another person's values, even if you don't connect to those values. Your value excavation must do no harm. Be sure that you create a "safe space" for your excavations, which means to set a nurturing ambience for your conversation that is friendly, confidential, puts the other person at ease, and engenders trust between you. Do not make this a test to pass. Instead, stay on a field trip, and avoid turning your excavation into an inquisition. Move at a slow pace, especially in the beginning.

You have named and empowered your values in part I. The more deeply you are connected to your values, the easier it is to excavate the values of others. You have also set the stage for your Value-Discovery Conversation and activated your field-trip mindset (exercise 19). Do what you can to provide fertile ground for a fruitful conversation, and make the other person comfortable so they feel free to share their ideas, stories, and issues. Embrace openness and curiosity with them. Excavating the values of others should be a natural process, so let it evolve naturally.

ENGAGE WITH OPENNESS AND CURIOSITY

Verbal and nonverbal acknowledgments let your coworker know you're listening and demonstrate that you're curious about what they're saying. This encourages them to speak from a deeper level of connection.

Verbal Acknowledgments

Inserting phrases of acknowledgment such as "Yes, I see" and "That's very interesting" encourages your coworker to say more. Feel these sentiments authentically rather than just paying lip service. Depending on whom you are talking with, if you genuinely feel excited or energized you can take it up a notch and use phrases such as "Wow, I get it" and "That's awesome – tell me more." These simple acknowledgments let your coworker know that you are listening to them powerfully.

Nonverbal Acknowledgments

We communicate nonverbally throughout a conversation. Being conscious of communicating positive acknowledgments via your body language sets the right mood for value excavation. An affirmative nod of the head, a slight lean in, eye contact, a smile... are all acknowledgments that can open up a conversation.

Ask Open-Ended Questions

First and foremost, asking questions invites the speaker to say more. Open-ended questions – ones that cannot be answered with a yes or no – indicate you are truly curious about what the person is saying. They allow them to go deeper into what they're thinking. The depth of the information allows for an open-ended answer that is often illuminating and, at times, unexpected. Questions that begin with *who, what, when, where, why,* and *how* open up the conversation.

When I first started coaching I found myself asking questions, but too often they elicited only yes or no answers, which limited the conversation. Working for over fifteen years as a certified coach has taught me to ask my Chemistry-Factor clients the kinds of questions that encourage and support them to say more. Even at the beginning of a session, instead of asking my client if they are having a good day, I ask them, "How is your day going?" This gets them thinking, eliciting a response that is more interesting and more revealing – perfect for excavating values.

LISTEN CLOSELY

When listening, most people focus on the topic being discussed. This prioritization of the content is understandable, but remember that in a Value-Discovery Conversation you are listening for *values*. This means that your listening should take you deeper into the content and alert you to how the speaker delivers the content.

At the content level, you focus deeply on your coworker's stories, viewpoints, topics, feelings, and ideas. At the speaking level, take note of the tone, presence, and feelings behind what is being said. By listening closely you collect the raw material from which you excavate values.

Since close listening reaps so many values, you want to do whatever you can to power it up. Here are some tips for listening:

Sharpen Your Focus

Staying focused during a Value-Discovery Conversation is critical to being able to listen closely. Sharpening your ability to stay focused is a skill you can practice. Try this meditation exercise:

EXERCISE 20
SHARPEN YOUR FOCUS: FINGERTIP MEDITATION

1. Sit in a comfortable position and relax your body while keeping your back straight.

2. Close your eyes and take a deep breath to settle you and your body into a meditative state.

3. Bring your hands together in prayer position in front of your chest.

4. Focus on the tips of your middle fingers and press them lightly together. Continue to both press them together and focus on that touch-point. Hold this focus as long as you can.

5. If your mind wanders, gently bring it back to the focus point of your middle fingertips touching.

6. Try to extend the time you can stay focused.

Setting a timer so you don't have to check to see how long you have meditated can help you meditate longer from one practice to the next.

Eliminate or Reduce External Distractions

Making the effort to eliminate or reduce external distractions before a Value-Discovery Conversation really pays off. For instance, arrange for someone to pick up your phone calls, choose a location with minimal noise, and close the door so others won't feel free to interrupt your conversation.

Minimize Internal Distractions

Your internal state can also distract your focus. When you're tired, your mind wanders to how you feel; when you're worried, your mind wanders to your worry. Put your internal distractions aside during the conversation. Exercise 11 in chapter 5, "Focus and Clear," is useful here.

Don't Veer Off into Judgment

It's very easy to let your critical mind enter the conversation and start passing judgment on what your coworker is saying. As much as possible, keep judgment out of the conversation. The less judgment, the more potential for value excavation. Remember, the end goal is authentic connection. Judgment is not part of that.

Don't Think about What You Want to Say

It's natural to focus on what you will say in response to what is being said. This distracts you from listening. Be truly interested in what your coworker has to say. If you then need some time to formulate your response, the well-listened-to person will be happy to wait for it whether it takes minutes or comes the next day.

Reinforce What Your Coworker Says by Repeating It to Yourself

Mentally repeating what is being said to you is a practice that can dramatically improve your listening skill. It might feel awkward at first, but with practice it becomes second nature. Meanwhile you will appreciate your improved listening skill, as will your partner in conversation.

EXCAVATE VALUES

In chapter 4 you learned to value-mine your values. Now you will take a similar approach to excavating the values of others. Remember that they are treasures. Dig carefully to keep the value intact and unharmed. You are not a construction worker; you're a scholar and explorer, unearthing treasures that are 24-karat gold for authentic connection.

Keep in mind that value excavation can be done during the conversation *and* afterward, in reflection. Reflection after any interaction is a great idea, but to boost your Chemistry Factor you specifically reflect on the *values* in evidence.

Create a Coworker's Value List (see appendix I or download it at www. thechemistryfactor.com/book) for each person with whom you have a Value-Discovery Conversation. This helps you remember the values you connect to with this person as well as the ones you don't connect to. Add to your Coworker's Values Lists whenever you discover new values.

The values you find are the treasures of your excavation and the elements you will use in value-matching. Learning to excavate values supercharges your ability to create powerful business relationships, and that is what the Chemistry Factor is all about.

Excavate Values from Conversation Content

As you listen closely during your Value-Discovery conversation, pay attention to specific stories, viewpoints, topics, and ideas. Consider the values that are revealed. Let this be a natural and intuitive process. Don't try to figure it out; just name and note the values that come to mind.

It's helpful to be able to both take and consult notes during the conversation. Since taking and consulting notes during business meetings is a common practice, doing this as part of your Value-Discovery Conversation should not be a challenge. You can use the "clean canvas" you created in exercise 19, "Set Your Field-Trip Mindset." If you have handy the Chemistry Factor Values Reference List, your Values Vault, and/or your Power Values List, you can easily checkmark which values come to mind as you listen without having to write them out.

As you have already discovered from mining your own values, stories are chock full of values. The plots themselves are useful for value discovery, as are the slant of the person's storytelling, the way the characters are described, and the style of the narration. All the elements of a story are fertile ground for evoking values.

Beyond the stories that your coworker tells, review all of the content spoken, because it provides even further clues to values. Naturally their viewpoints on various topics reveal values that are important to them. For instance, if someone believes in equal rights for all, it may come from their value of fairness and/or justice. If they are focused on retirement fund choices, they might be expressing values of security and/or planning.

In reviewing your coworker's ideas, you can learn how they process information and make it their own. This, too, reveals values. For instance, when offered an investment tip, one person might see it as an opportunity while another sees it as a risky venture. In both cases, how the person sees the information reveals their values at that time.

As you excavate for values, it's not so much about identifying the perfect or "right" values as it is about identifying the values that *seem important* to your coworker. This is the right place to start when value-matching and creating chemistry with this person. Despite this deep dive into values, *don't lose track of the ultimate goal of creating powerful business relationships.*

Afterward, take a few minutes to reflect on the conversation. If you did not take notes, write down the values you excavated while they are still fresh in your mind. Let go of any that do not seem to fit. Consider other values that might be more deeply woven into what the speaker said. Use your notes, your Chemistry Factor Values Reference List, your Values Vault, and your Power Values List.

Excavate Values from Your Coworker's Tells

There are three tells that assist value excavation:

1. **The tone of your coworker's voice:** The tone of voice reveals a lot about them. For example, confidence can be an important value for success, and your coworker's tone can reveal how well they have embraced the value of confidence. Does their tone display true confidence? When a person truly owns a value, it shows up in all kinds of ways – subtly or boldly, consciously or subconsciously. Think about how just "hello" can be said in many different tones, and what those tones reveal about your coworker. When you go into the office tomorrow morning, pay attention to each person's "Good morning." Notice what values are tagging along with or absent from each person's greeting.

2. **Their presence:** Presence, or body language, says a great deal about a person's values, and since these nonverbal cues are often displayed unconsciously, they can be very revealing. As a person speaks you can see what kind of energy lies behind what they're saying based on the stance of their body. For example, if they say something that indicates a value of honesty while standing upright and making direct eye contact with you, it shows how true this value feels for them; if their body is slouched and they cannot maintain eye contact, it shows that there is something off about what they're saying, and that they're possibly not connecting to honesty.

3. **The feelings behind their words:** As you experienced in the Life-Story Values exercises, every sentence in a conversation contains values to discover. Picture your coworker's sentences as waves that wash over you. In these waves are values you can feel that tell you a lot about the other person and are important to identify.

   As the sentence waves come in, listen to your gut feeling or sixth sense to detect your coworker's values on an intuitive level. Take notes of these "felt" values and name them when possible.

   After your Value-Discovery Conversation, take the time to replay the conversation in your mind. Notice which sentences were "big waves" that your coworker obviously felt comfortable speaking. Those sentences reveal values that are very important to them.

Recall any points in the conversation when you did not feel comfortable. These indicate that the speaker was disconnected from a value that is important to them. For example, an employee tells you how confident she is about taking on a new task. Everything she says confirms her confidence, and her tone and presence are positive. Yet as you feel the sentence waves, there is something in the way of her confidence. This gut feeling is worth looking at.

In one such case, my client's employee did indeed have a concern. She felt completely confident about her ability to perform the task and complete the project, but she was worried about some trouble her daughter was having at school, and the missing piece in her confidence was how she would be able to deal with that while taking on this new task. Once this fear was exposed, my client was happy to give her some flexible hours for her daughter's sake. Her confidence soared as well as her productivity. She connected with my client on many other values including support and empathy, strengthening their powerful relationship.

Once you open to this level of understanding and learn to trust the intuitive level of your value excavation, it will feel natural.

After the Value-Discovery Conversation, take a few minutes and reflect on your coworker's tone, presence, and feelings. Add any additional excavated values to their Coworker's Values List. (See appendix I or download it at www.thechemistryfactor.com/book.) These are your treasures. They are the keys to your authentic connection with this person. They are the elements of the chemistry you will use to create a powerful business relationship.

FORMAL AND INFORMAL DISCOVERY

As mentioned earlier, your Value-Discovery Conversations can be formal or informal. You have both formal and informal conversations with the people you encounter regularly at work, and your connections with them come from both.

A formal conversation could be a meeting you set up to discuss your relationship with a specific person. You can be very direct in your exploration of values in such a conversation to find matching values with them.

A more informal Value-Discovery Conversation can happen at any meeting, or can even be a brief conversation in the cafeteria. Don't judge these conversations as lightweight in terms of value excavation. Imagine your coworker telling you a few stories from their weekend, and you can see how these stories are likely to be rich in values. Every time you cross paths with someone, there is an opportunity for value excavation!

Your Value-Discovery Conversations can be in person, face to face via online conferencing, or by phone. There are advantages and disadvantages to each. If by phone, you can more easily take notes and use your values lists. In-person and online conversations allow you the extra advantage of seeing the other person's body language.

EXERCISE 21
HAVE AN *INFORMAL* VALUE-DISCOVERY CONVERSATION

1. For your first conversation, choose someone with whom you already feel comfortable and hold an informal conversation, even if it's just a brief exchange in the hallway. Use the strategies described above, excavating values from both conversation content *and* your coworker's tells.

2. Take some time to reflect on the values available for excavation, and create a Coworker's Values List for this person to record the excavated values.

EXERCISE 22
HAVE A *FORMAL* VALUE-DISCOVERY CONVERSATION

1. Choose a context in which to suggest the meeting to the person. This can range from a direct approach to providing another reason for the meeting and planning to excavate values during the meeting.

   • An example of the direct approach: Tell your coworker you want to get to know them better and improve your connection with them. Let them know before the meeting, or at the beginning of the meeting, that you want to explore the values you share. You can modify this approach to fit the situation.

- An example of a less direct approach: Set up a meeting that's needed in the normal course of your work. During the meeting weave your values excavation into the agenda. Asking for your coworker's opinion about a meeting topic is a great way to discover some of their values.

2. Prepare for the value-discovery aspect of the meeting. If taking a less direct approach, consider how to integrate it into the meeting, and definitely plan on some reflection time after the meeting so you can focus on the values available for excavation.

3. Use the strategies described in this chapter to excavate values from both conversation content *and* your coworker's tells.

4. Create a Coworker's Values List for this person and record the excavated values.

MORE PRACTICE

Again, practice! You know what practice makes... so as well as practicing your value excavation in all your conversations, you can also try the following exercise:

EXERCISE 23
PRACTICE VALUE EXCAVATION

Value-mining for your own values is admittedly easier than excavating for another person's values. When mining your values you can review content again and again, whereas in conversation with a coworker you only have one opportunity to dig up values. This exercise is a specific way to practice for Value-Discovery Conversations.

Listen to radio programs and watch television shows, social media programs, or movies to extract values from a chosen character or speaker. Use not only what the person says but also notice their tone and presence. Let the sentence waves inform your intuition as to the person's values, and determine whether or not you connect to those values. Practice writing them down and reflecting after watching or listening to the show. Practicing can unearth more of your own values as well.

IT'S AN ONGOING PROCESS

Value discovery is an ongoing and multifaceted process. The best chemistry is created when you continue to excavate values and when you excavate in a variety of ways. Most important, have fun. Getting to know someone through the lens of values is rewarding in all kinds of ways. Each step of the Chemistry Factor is beneficial on its own, and truly powerful when added to the others.

SEVEN

MATCH VALUES

Einstein gave us the definition of insanity as "doing the same thing over and over again and expecting a different result." How many of your business relationships fit that definition? How much of an effort are you putting in to improve them? How many of your relationships work even though you're using the same old value perspectives and you haven't taken the relationship to the next level?

In business, leaders succeed by constantly challenging their perspectives to discover new success strategies. *Since*

*a company's biggest asset is its people, using authentic con-
nections to inspire greater business relationships is essential in
developing those new winning strategies.*

Your Values Vault is filled and you have learned how to
use Value-Discovery Conversations to excavate the values of
the people you want to connect with. It is now time to match
values and authentically connect with your coworkers. In
other words, it's time to create some chemistry.

USING YOUR CHEMISTRY FACTOR

By now you should feel the energy of empowering your
values, and you have learned to identify the values of others.
Now you will develop the skill of value-matching, which allows you to quickly and easily connect on an authentic level
with anyone you choose to. This skill can greatly improve
longstanding relationships, difficult and/or contentious relationships, and new relationships. It helps you open the doors
to even more powerful business relationships.

DEEP AND POWERFUL

The Chemistry Factor deepens your personal connections
with people at work because it is *values-based.* The value-
matching step is important because you are consciously
and proactively choosing to deepen the connection. There
are pessimists out there with small Values Vaults and little
chance of connecting their values with the people they work
with. Sometimes it seems they look for mismatches and
feed off negative, disconnected energy. They may get the job
done, but at the cost of added stress that drains their energy
and limits success. You, on the other hand, are primed and
ready to find value matches that increase your energy and
inspire greater success in your career.

POSSIBLE DRAWBACKS

Before we ignite your authentic connections, let's look at two common concerns you might have: 1) the perceived need to compromise your values in order to find a match, and 2) being the one who does all the "work."

Compromising a value in order to match it with another's often shows up as the indignant question "Why do I have to change my values to connect with someone else? Why can't they change their values to connect with me?" To be clear about the issue of compromise: You do not have to, nor should you, compromise or change your values to find a match. The Chemistry Factor does not ask you to change your values. In fact, I want you to empower only those values that are authentic and genuine within you. You can fill your Values Vault with a variety of values that allow you to find value matches with any person you want to connect with.

It is possible that with a few individuals it will be hard – at least initially – to find a value in yourself that matches powerfully with one of theirs. But this is a rare circumstance, especially as you get more proficient at activating your values and recognizing the values of the person you want to authentically connect with. But even a weak value match is better than no connection at all. It eventually can be the bridge that over time allows you to find stronger values to match, expanding your Values Vault while knocking down the walls of disconnection.

Now let's consider the second worry: the "work" always falling on you. Begin by considering this issue as a worst-case scenario. You did the work – you found a value to match and your relationship with that person is better – but they seem to be relying on you to continue to find ways to connect. Who cares? The Chemistry Factor is not work in the traditional sense, and you are benefiting in so many ways, so being the proactive one shouldn't feel like an onerous obligation. In most cases, once you open up a relationship with some shared values, the other person will change in ways that make them a partner in value-matching. The chemistry is addictive!

I remember working as a recruiter with a controller whom I found to be very difficult. We succeeded in finding candidates for his openings, but he was very impersonal and disorganized. On several occasions he forgot our appointments, which was very uncomfortable for everyone involved. I was happy to see him leave the company.

Years later we found ourselves working together again when he was at a different company as finance director. We had both grown; he was more comfortable in this new company culture and I was more conscious about how to authentically connect with people I work with.

We actually enjoyed working together the second time around. The first time we communicated from disconnected values, which created a stressful relationship. I never really tried to authentically connect with him because I was worried he would stand up another candidate. He shared with me that he had not been happy in the old job, which resulted in stress. I had not yet developed the Chemistry-Factor approach, and we could have avoided a lot of grief had we worked from common values in our first encounter.

THE TIME IS NOW

This is that exciting moment for a chemist, when you are ready to mix two elements together to create a formula. You are mixing your value with your coworker's value to create an authentically connected relationship. In the movie version, this chemistry experiment could explode. In this Chemistry-Factor scenario, however, you are well prepared and greater success is waiting for you. The value-match spark turns into enjoyable fireworks, not real kabooms.

Let's activate the formula.

VALUE-MATCHING

There are three steps in value-matching:

1. Finding a shared value to match from your Co-worker's Values List (See appendix I)

2. Connecting to the value by empowering it

3. Authentically connecting with your coworker through the perspective of the chosen value

Let's look at each step on its own:

FIND A SHARED VALUE TO MATCH

In chapters 4, 5, and 6 you filled your Values Vault and used Value-Discovery Conversations to identify the values of others. Now it's time to find a shared value by simply comparing your Values Vault with the values of your coworker. There will be values that you do not share, but there are also ones that you do.

One of my coaching clients complained to me about a vice president she was working with. She felt her relationship with him was far from powerful. Together we searched for a value she could match with one of his.

The next time she met with him she realized that the value they had often used in common – strategic thinking

– was no longer connecting them as it used to. It was now predictable common ground and provided less spark than it had when they had worked together to rebuild their production department. The department had improved its communication and delivery timings to everyone's satisfaction.

My client used the Value-Discovery Conversation approach the next time they spoke, and she heard an optimistic tone in the VP's voice. That was a value she was able to easily connect to. The value of optimism rekindled their relationship.

Connecting to the value of optimism was the bridge that grew their relationship, and she was able to add more matching values including recognition, enthusiasm, and bottom-lining. When the VP became the senior vice president, you can guess who took over his position: my client.

There are several ways to find a shared value. Knowing the values on each side of this formula, you can find those that both of you honor. The more specific you are about identifying the values, the easier it is to find a shared value that truly matches.

CONNECT TO THE VALUE

Create the best chance for a powerful connection with your coworker by making sure you are connected to the chosen value. The deeper your connection to and understanding of the value, the better the match. If your connection to the value feels solid, go to the next step. If not, consider one of two options: 1) choose another value that you feel more connected to, or 2) take the chosen value through the empower-and-connect process you learned in chapter

5. Choose whichever option feels best in the situation, as neither is better than the other.

AUTHENTICALLY CONNECT THROUGH THE PERSPECTIVE OF THE CHOSEN VALUE

Robert was an executive vice president in charge of the digital department of a large agency. He was very skilled at building relationships, and started to employ the Chemistry Factor as part of his leadership skills. He practiced empowering his values, which came in handy when unexpected chaos disrupted the office, and his calm personality helped him connect with others.

A client's advertising program went haywire. A social media event that was supposed to reap huge numbers of potential clients visiting the site was not working – there was a glitch in the system. The client was angry, and so was Robert's CEO. Robert was at a loss; calm wasn't making it.

Remembering values that he had in common with his CEO, Robert consciously empowered the value of common sense. He confidently told the CEO that the problem would be quickly fixed and the client would be compensated for the loss of information. That was exactly what the CEO wanted to hear – a clear path to correcting the error.

Everyone involved was called to a meeting with a clear understanding of how to rectify the problem. The client appreciated the dedication, action, and honesty that came from Robert and his CEO, and their relationship became even stronger than it was before. Connecting to common sense quickly inspired the agency to turn a failure into success – a peak moment of accomplishment in a trying situation.

By authentically connecting with your coworker through the perspective of the chosen value, you're basing the connection on a commonality. If you are willing to invoke it, the power of a shared value is immense. You will find that a shared value can provide an ample platform for agreement and collaboration, resulting in the kinds of powerful relationships that lead to your work and career success. This platform becomes a win-win-win situation for you, your coworkers, and your clients.

One shared value can break through many areas of disagreement or difference. This puts you at the best end of the perspective where, despite any disagreement, you are willing and likely to find common ground from the perspective of the shared value. Even a small connection can allow things to move forward and out of stalemate.

One of my coaching clients, Randall, ran a monthly board of directors meeting. Everyone on the board dreaded the meetings because one member was consistently defensive about every issue. In fact, she seemed to relish her habit of taking up opposing views. Randall thought her defensiveness might be rooted in a belief that she was not being heard, so before and during the next meeting he made sure to authentically connect with her through the value of powerful listening. As it turned out she still disagreed with Randall and others regarding two of the five issues discussed that day, but she expressed her disagreement in a much calmer way, allowing for great compromises to be worked out.

After the meeting the other board members all commented privately to Randall about how successful the meeting had been. They did not know about his secret

Chemistry-Factor technique, but they did see the results of authentic connection.

AUTHENTICITY AND CHEMICAL SPARK

You have chosen a value to match and have empowered it. Now it's time to match the value and authentically connect. There is no need to make this more complicated than it is. You've given the value a prominent place in this moment, and this "presencing" of the value anchors the connection in authenticity. You can now let go of other excavated values that do not further the connection.

To complete the connection, approach and interact with your coworker through the perspective of the chosen value. Just as a different lens does not change what you see but brings to light different characteristics of it, this seemingly small shift can result in amazing chemistry. This is the spark of the authentic connection.

There are various levels to this spark. Your use of the value's perspective might be subtle, shifting your thinking about and communication with your coworker. For example, you might inspire them by speaking in terms of the matching value of mentoring rather than speaking of discipline.

I had a client who often managed her staff with the value of independence. It was a DNA Value of hers that she always yearned for. Working with me she came to realize that whenever she called someone to her office they were afraid they were going to be disciplined. Her value of giving her staff independence made it time-consuming for them to figure things out on their own, so when she called them to her office it was most likely to ask them why the delay. She was giving them enough rope to hang themselves.

She learned that she was too attached to the value of independence. She felt that by discovering answers for themselves her employees would experience better learning; they wanted to learn as much as she wanted them to, but her method reduced productivity.

Using the Chemistry Factor Program, she remembered a peak moment in her life when she opened her first checking account with her father. Without his guidance she would have been very insecure about asking the right questions and taking the right steps. It was a fond memory because her father took the time for her as a mentor. She decided she would do the same thing for her staff.

She empowered her value of mentoring by remembering her first checking account. That mentoring perspective led her to arrange a set time, most every day, to be available for questions from her staff. She explained her reasons for wanting them to learn independently, and they were now able to see independence as a positive challenge rather than a burden. Her employees now looked forward to visits in her office, authentically connecting with her as a mentor. The result was they created greater productivity and support in the department.

You can also speak directly with your coworker about the value itself to spark connection. One of my coaching clients, a CEO, won a major production project for his company. He told his employee she was chosen to run the job because they shared the value of accountability. He believed that a strong sense of accountability would keep this project on track, and he was right. The project went extremely well, bringing in new business from the client. Beyond the success of the project, their direct discussion about the value of accountability set up a lasting and rewarding Chemistry-Factor relationship that continues to grow with additional value matches. By recognizing and verbalizing the value directly, my client's employee felt seen and appreciated, and was inspired to do great work for her boss, never wanting to let him down.

EXERCISE 24
VALUE-MATCHING

1. Choose a coworker with whom you have had a Value-Discovery Conversation. I suggest starting with someone you already have a good relationship with and trying to connect to a new value that you haven't matched with before. Once you start experiencing authentic connection it's easier to connect in more challenging relationships.

2. Choose a shared value and empower it.

3. Match values by connecting with your coworker through the perspective of the chosen value, igniting authentic connection with that person.

4. Enjoy and continue to build the powerful relationship that value-matching creates.

The more practiced you are at value excavation, the easier it is to value-match on the spot during your Value-Discovery Conversation.

VALUE-MATCHING TIPS

VISUALIZATION

To approach and interact with the person using the value you have chosen to connect through, prepare by visualizing how they manifest that value in their life. What was the instance that had you excavate this value in your conversation with them? How did it connect with you? This preparation does not need to be long or drawn out. The visualization prepares you to naturally associate this value with this person.

THE ART OF VALUE-MATCHING

Value-matching is an art. Don't worry if your first attempt at a match doesn't work. In fact, you might try several values before you find a great match.

The good news is that you will not only *know* it when you find a good match, but you will also *feel the spark*. You might not have labeled it before reading this book, but you have surely felt the spark that marks the beginning of authentic connection in both your personal life and professional life. It's that feeling of inspiration that I wrote about at the beginning of the book. Enjoy learning the art of value-matching to create authentic connection, and appreciate that you have honed a new skill.

THINK LONG TERM

You have experienced the powerful feeling of being in an authentic relationship in which both of you feel heard, seen, and accepted for who you truly are; you feel respected and cared about; and you feel a connection – sometimes one that you can't even explain. Quite honestly, it just feels great.

While you can feel the rewards of the Chemistry Factor as soon as you start working with it, you can also look forward to the long-term success of a work life and career full of these authentic relationships. Be confident that the long-term benefits of powerful business relationships will show up for you, sometimes when you least expect them. They result in great business karma.

CURRENT OR NEW RELATIONSHIPS

If you're value-matching in a current relationship, be aware that the other person might have this relationship set in a groove and might be surprised by or not respond to the new avenue of connection you're forging. Keep trying. After two or three attempts to value-match without feeling the spark of authentic connection, try matching another value that you share with this person. (We will review this in chapter 8 under the heading "Shift Values.")

I have a friend from my school days, Peter, who is a go-to colleague with whom I share many of my career decisions. We started out as two guys focused on changing the world, achieving great things, and enjoying life. In fact, I find myself slipping right back into those fresh-out-of-school and early-career values every time I speak with Peter.

When I started developing the Chemistry Factor, I became more conscious of the values embedded in every interaction Peter and I have. Some of our common values include being open-minded, being analytical, and appreciating powerful communication. These values can show up in our discussions about current events, in which we often agree – but not always. It's interesting that I now find those disagreements rewarding.

Our relationship has deepened over time, expanding well beyond the values we shared as kids. Expanding our authentic connection has made us as close as brothers even though for many years we did it unconsciously. Whenever we find ourselves disconnecting we go to a value that reconnects us rather quickly. But we have so much in common that this is rarely necessary.

You have the same opportunity with any person with whom you want to build a relationship. It can start slowly – Peter and I did get into a fight or two when we were younger; but if you stay dedicated to authentically connecting with those you work with, you will achieve amazing results in your career and life.

If you're value-matching in a new relationship, there are fewer value-excavation treasures available. But that can be positive, as there are also fewer values to disconnect you. Choosing a potential shared value might involve some guesswork. No problem. If the first value you try doesn't work after two or three cracks at it, try another. Keep trying and be persistent until you strike gold.

THE
CHEMISTRY
FACTOR
PROGRAM

III.

CREATE POWERFUL
BUSINESS RELATIONSHIPS

EIGHT

MASTER YOUR CHEMISTRY FACTOR

Let's imagine the sparks of authentic connection as the fireworks on the Fourth of July. I admit that fireworks still thrill me – as do authentic connections. My favorite part is the grand finale when the whole sky is lit up with multiple fireworks all at once.

In Chemistry-Factor terms, while each values-based authentic connection is something to celebrate, the *pièce de résistance* is the powerful business relationships they create. It is these business relationships that pay great dividends in your current and future career.

Mastering your Chemistry Factor gives you additional skills for creating higher-level business relationships. This chapter begins with some advanced value-matching techniques that allow you to easily shift values until you find one that truly ignites an authentic connection. I also share additional tips for using your Chemistry Factor and further information on mindset, practice, and strategy. When you add everything together you have mastered the art of authentic connection.

ADVANCED VALUE-MATCHING

Shifting values was discussed in chapter 5 as a technique to use when you are connecting to your own values. Shifting values when value-matching with others is an advanced technique that gives you flexibility and assures amazing connection. Another advanced connection technique is *value expansion.* This is a way to deal with the multifaceted nature of values.

SHIFT VALUES

As discussed earlier, you might choose a value to match with someone, but when implemented it just doesn't take. When this happens you want to be able to shift values.

The goal is not to make a given value match by forcing it; that does not result in authentic connection. The goal is to find a value that is an easy match and allows powerful authentic connection to occur naturally. This is chemistry at its best.

If you find that the first value you choose is not the best value match, it is time to shift. Remember you are not aiming for just "ho-hum" connection; when a value match does not click in easily, try another one.

EXERCISE 25
SHIFT VALUES WHILE VALUE-MATCHING

1. Choose your shift-to value. Assuming you have already empowered it, connect to this value. (See exercise 16.) If you have created a connection trigger for the value, use it to make the connection. (See exercise 17.)

2. Once connected to the shift-to value, let the first value go.

3. Authentically connect with the other person through the perspective of the new value.

If your shift-to value is not connecting, try again after using exercise 11, "Focus and Clear," or shift to yet another value. The beauty of this process is that you have many Power Values to choose from.

VALUE EXPANSION

Certain situations require a more specific value than the one you first chose to connect through. This is when value expansion is most helpful. When a value is "stretched out," you can see how the core value has other values as roots. Expansion into the specificity of the roots adds meaning to any value.

Values Are Multifaceted

It's true – no one value is one value. Thinking of them as singular concepts makes connecting and staying connected easier, but can feel limiting. When working with values at an advanced level, it is sometimes useful to think in terms of value expansion.

Start with a given value. You will notice that in defining the value, there are additional specific values (roots) that more deeply define and expand the core value.

Core Value + Roots

A core value can multiply into many values, giving you more flexibility in your value-matching ventures and making your value more specific and clear. By thinking in terms of value expansion, you acknowledge and use the multifaceted nature of values.

For example, a senior director was having a difficult time with a client services supervisor regarding the value of collaboration. All her staff members working on a request-for-pitch assignment were collaborating to formulate the presentation except this supervisor. The director was annoyed by this but instead of making this supervisor wrong for his lack of collaboration on the pitch, she decided to look at other values she could associate with collaboration that were roots of that value.

She thought of values such as support, friendship, and mentoring, and chose to empower support, which was one of her Power Values. She asked him, "What can I do to help you on this new pitch assignment?" The supervisor began feeling more connected and shared with her that he was overwhelmed by another assignment. He wanted separation from the group to complete it, but was uncomfortable about saying so. He had felt wrong about not collaborating but thought his excuse would make the situation worse.

The value of support can work both in receiving and giving. As soon as the senior director connected to the value of support with her supervisor, collaboration began to take place. Other members of the team committed to supporting him with his assignment, allowing his stress to dissipate. He was now inspired to work with the team on the pitch, and the work he had to complete was done quickly with the support he was given.

The power of authentic connection improved the productivity for everyone in the group. The work at hand for their new business presentation was enthusiastically completed, and they were well prepared for the client's visit and energized to take on their next assignments. Chemistry-Factor magic!

EXERCISE 26
VALUE EXPANSION

1. Choose a value you are considering for a value match with a coworker.

2. Write down the core value, then list the root values that come to mind as you think about the core value. Don't judge the values you are writing down; just write them down. (You can use the Chemistry Factor Values Reference List in appendix A to help you come up with root values.)

3. Choose three root values from your list and fill in the template below:

    Core Value / Root Value / Root Value / Root Value

    In this way you can see how each of the root values clarifies the core value yet stands on its own.

4. Choose one of the root values to value-match with your coworker.

5. Shift your value-matching to the chosen value.

More about Value Expansion

When choosing a root value, look for one that clarifies and adds to your original core value. When you're writing down root values you may include some that are important to you but do not belong in the particular connection situation.

Root values do not have to fit "inside" each other like Russian nesting dolls or be connected in a logical way. Choose the root value that most brightly highlights the meaning of the core value.

Any given value can be a core value and/or a root value. Accepting this premise allows you to stop your logical, critical mind from making it more difficult to narrow down your value options than it needs to be. Don't make discovering root values too complicated by trying to find the perfect fit. The simpler the value the easier it is to create a great value match that leads to authentic connection and a powerful business relationship. The desired outcome is not a perfect value; it's authentic connection and powerful business relationships.

CHEMISTRY-FACTOR TIPS

The Chemistry Factor is bucking a trend in this world. With technology's increasing hold on our attention, pure and wonderful connection can become lost. This means that your Chemistry Factor will stand out and shine a very favorable spotlight on you.

Your ability to create authentic connections and outstanding business relationships is going to be highly valued, making people feel heard and respected for who they are. So let's look at a few factors to consider in the Chemistry Factor Program.

FAKING IT DOES NOT WORK

You can't fake chemistry. You will know the effort is insincere and the other person will eventually know it as well. It might not happen on the spot; you both might believe in the chemistry of the connection, but on reflection the shine will wear away to resentful disconnection.

Who hasn't faked chemistry at work – smiling on the outside with the person who shot down your idea in a meeting while churning on the inside; showing enthusiasm for the boss's project while you're thinking it's a waste of time; or just working with someone you would prefer not to and stifling your notions that they're too loud, too slow, too this or that? We do it either knowingly or unconsciously because we're numb to the disconnected relationship, taking it in stride.

In fact, if you think about it, faking chemistry, no matter how effective at first, eventually magnifies the disconnection. And we have all experienced someone telling us one thing while we get a strong sense that the truth is something else. It is the worst stereotype of the salesperson saying whatever they must say to get the sale. They're not trying to sell you because they believe in the product; something inside you just knows that what they really care about is their commission.

REACHING OUT MATTERS

Reaching out to others from the depth of value-matching is essential to creating Chemistry-Factor relationships. The more willing you are to reach out to people, the better for your Chemistry Factor.

It would be easy to dismiss taking the time to reach out because of your already busy schedule. But don't assume that reaching out is about long, in-depth conversations. You can show interest in someone, have a brief but deep interaction, and cover lots of Chemistry-Factor ground in a short time.

MINDSET

The right mindset sets the stage for success in any practice or with any skill. The following mindset tips make your chemistry more potent and its spark more brilliant.

Stay Conscious and Proactive

Value-matching itself calls on you to be conscious and proactive in your interactions. At the mastery level you pay specific attention to being conscious and proactive about creating Chemistry-Factor relationships with as many people as possible.

Before being introduced to the Chemistry Factor, you might have created business relationships on a spontaneous and unconscious trial-and-error level using an autopilot approach. The Chemistry-Factor approach calls for being more mindful and bringing consciousness to each relationship. This can be difficult at first, but through mastery it becomes second nature. By making this ability a conscious one and taking it seriously as a career advantage, you are truly powering it up.

The goals are to keep the process active and to allow it to become a natural part of your interactions with others, similar to the way your body takes to exercise. At first you want to consciously add exercise to your daily routine. By being proactive, exercise will eventually become a natural and desired part of your daily activities.

As you use your Chemistry-Factor skills you will notice two things. One is that creating a space of safety and trust for each relationship is critical in reaching the depths of values-based connection; be proactive on this front. The second is that Chemistry-Factor relationships, because they are both their own reward and very rewarding in terms of your career, become self-perpetuating. The more Chemistry-Factor relationships you create, the more you will want to continue to connect; and the more authentic your connections, the more authenticity you will offer and seek.

Let Go of Old Stories and Beliefs

Old stories and beliefs can be the wreckages that obstruct your ability to create values-based authentic relationships. So it's important to identify and release them when appropriate.

John was a business owner who had an old story in his head that if he got too friendly with his staff it would muddle his relationships and make it difficult for him to refuse requests for raises. Digging into this story he discovered it was originally "planted" when he started his first business and was struggling to make payroll. The less friendly he was with his staff, the easier it was to say no.

He later realized that by authentically connecting with his staff and improving his leadership skills, their productivity improved. He also learned that in an authentically connected company people are so comfortable that they will accept less than market value for their services because they enjoy the company culture and look forward to staying together. I've known many people who stayed with a company for years, making less than they would if they moved on, because they liked working there so much. John learned that he could both save money and increase productivity by creating powerful business relationships.

Old beliefs can also create obstacles to fully embracing your Chemistry Factor. For example, if you believe that anyone at your company who is technically "below" you in the hierarchy should adopt your values, this belief will greatly limit your ability to value-match with your staff. For one thing, this attitude about employee management is not compatible with the Chemistry Factor; but furthermore it restricts the values you can choose from to create a Chemistry-Factor relationship. Making people wrong because they don't share values with you is a toxic formula for disconnection.

Believe in the Match

Believe in the value matches you make. Belief is a powerful motivator, and when you're firing up the chemistry in a relationship it is a very important element. When you trust in your value matches, you're accelerating your ability to create powerful business relationships. When you're authentically connected, belief and action come easily.

Remember that the simplest shared values can be extremely powerful in creating Chemistry-Factor relationships. I had a client who shared the value of timeliness with me. It completely delighted her that when she called me for her coaching session at exactly the top of the hour I would answer on the first ring. Her acknowledgment of my timeliness made me happy as well. It was one of those win-win situations that started our sessions on the right footing. It's inspiring to share something as deep and important as a value.

Commit

Abraham Lincoln said, "Commitment is what transforms a promise into a reality." For the Chemistry Factor to be a reality in your work and career life, simply commit to it.

There is no way around this. So I make a commitment to you: I am committed to bringing the Chemistry Factor to the world of business. Through my coaching and speaking I want to change how we work together – in our companies and in our careers in general. I commit to your greater success and the enrichment of your Chemistry-Factor path. I am here to help you ignite your Chemistry Factor.

PRACTICE, PRACTICE, PRACTICE

The more you use your Chemistry Factor, the easier it is to use it and the more effective it becomes.

- Use it at work, formally or informally.

- Connect with everyone from the receptionist to the CEO to strengthen your company culture.

- Enjoy greater business success by training everyone from your upper-level managers to your front-line employees to ignite their Chemistry Factors.

- Your bottom line improves when your company becomes a Chemistry-Factor company.

- Use your ability to create Chemistry-Factor relationships to change the speed and trajectory of your career.

- Practice naming, empowering, and connecting to your values; stay current with the values in your Values Vault; and consistently update your Power Values List.

- Practice the value-matching that creates Chemistry-Factor relationships using both values that you have matched with someone before and values you're matching for the first time.

- Continue to excavate values even after you've established chemistry with a coworker. Remember that every conversation you have with someone is an opportunity to discover more about their values.

In his book *Mastery*, George Leonard describes mastery as a point at which you make something "easy and pleasurable through instruction and practice." This is exactly what you want to do with your Chemistry Factor – make it easy and pleasurable. Easy and pleasurable come through when you are consciously connected to your values.

Integrating the Chemistry Factor into your activities every day is the best use of this skill. The more your Chemistry Factor is just part of how you communicate and develop relationships with your coworkers, the more natural and powerful it is.

Steady attention to the basic elements of the Chemistry Factor Program is essential in creating powerful business relationships and greater business success.

YOUR CHEMISTRY-FACTOR STRATEGY
KEEP TRACK – DATA ANALYTICS

Good chemists keep track of their work. They record elements used, conditions of the experiment, and resulting outcomes. With this data they analyze what worked and what didn't. They spot trends and highlight actions. They identify the elements that work and those that do not. They try new formulas to accomplish even more powerful outcomes. Most important, they continually repeat their success, making what looks extraordinary today look ordinary tomorrow.

You, too, will want to keep track of your Chemistry-Factor work, analyzing the elements you use (values) and their desired outcomes (Chemistry-Factor relationships).

Human interaction can be an inaccurate science, which is why I think of it as an art and a science. Every interaction you have in your pursuit of authentic connections is an "experiment," with some outcomes being more predictable than others. So keeping track of your Chemistry-Factor work helps you make authentic connection more perpetual and predictable.

To do this, simply keep a notebook, journal, or computer document in which you record your values explorations and the value-matching aspects of your relationships in both your company and your career. Here are the categories you will want to keep track of:

- Your Values Vault and Power Values List

- The excavated values of your coworkers – the Coworker's Values Lists

- The value matches you have made, both successfully and not.

- The benefits at your company and in your career of creating values-based Chemistry-Factor relationships.

STAY CURRENT

The second part of your Chemistry-Factor strategy is to stay current. Continue to deepen your connections to your values. I suggest you set aside ten minutes of dedicated time each day to update your value discoveries and reinforce what you've already learned. During your commute is a great time to do this work, but it can be done at home, at the office, or even during leisure time. Those ten minutes a day are a small price to pay for powerful business relationships and the great success they bring you.

Mark your calendar for monthly deeper reviews of your Power Values List and your Values Vault. Add values that are currently resonating with you, and replace those that are not as on-target for you right now with ones that are. Don't be concerned that you will forget the ones you replace; it's like riding a bicycle: once you have empowered them it takes little effort to retrieve them.

Stay current in appreciating how your Chemistry Factor benefits your work life and career. Keep the chemistry moving forward. Reinforce successful value-match connections. Continue to excavate values from your coworkers and hone your value-shifting skill so it flows smoothly when needed. A value match is not a one-time action, and new value matches are invigorating and exciting, so go for the gold.

EPILOGUE

EXPAND THE POWER

To expand the power of your Chemistry Factor, start by enjoying yourself, the connections you're making, and the wonderful transformations taking place in your business relationships. Then broaden the reach of your Chemistry Factor.

ENJOY YOUR CHEMISTRY

How can you not have fun? When you are consciously connected to your values, joy is a natural result. It's energizing and inspiring. You get to be a creative chemist, and your ultimate results are powerful relationships in your business and career. Even the process itself is fun: you get to fill your Values Vault with treasures, empower your values, use your conversations to discover the values of your coworkers, then ignite the chemistry and enjoy greater success!

BUILD YOUR AUTHENTIC-RELATIONSHIP NETWORK

The connections you create using your Chemistry Factor provide a mutually empowered network of relationships where you work, and the result is greater success for everyone. This network inspires your day. Imagine enthusiastically rising out of bed and looking forward to going to work. Your office is now a place where business relationships inspire you to take action and thwart indecision, empowered by your values and being able to authentically connect with anyone you want to.

Chemistry-Factor relationships are a win-win-win for you, the people you work with, and your company! Power up your day, every day!

SHARE AUTHENTIC CONNECTION WITH OTHERS

When others in your office begin to create authentic-connection relationships, the Chemistry Factor magnifies within the company. Sharing this gift of creating powerful business relationships makes it easier to build them. The greater the support for the Chemistry Factor, the greater your company's success.

EMBRACE YOUR POWERFUL SUCCESS

The true benefit of the Chemistry Factor is your success. By using your Chemistry Factor as one of your success tools, you create greater success. This powerful success is real! Believe in it! Be open to receiving it! Know that you deserve it!

EXPAND THE POWER

The Chemistry Factor has taught you how to create powerful business relationships at work. The next step is to expand this chemistry to your network outside your office. Develop Chemistry-Factor relationships with your customers, vendors, LinkedIn network, other business associates, outside contractors – the possibilities are endless. This can take your success in business to levels beyond any big-picture goals you currently imagine!

Finally, expand your success into even more powerful success by adding chemistry to your personal relationships, too – all of them, from your closest friends and family for whom you may struggle to find time, to the smile you share with a stranger on the street. Reach that moment when igniting your Chemistry Factor becomes second nature to you! It will bring joy, happiness, and the power of authentic connection to your whole life!

APPENDICES

APPENDIX A
Chemistry Factor Values Reference List

Abstract thinking

Abundance

Acceptance

Accessibility

Accomplishment

Accountability

Accuracy

Achievement

Acknowledgment

Action

Activeness

Adaptability

Adoration

Advancement

Adventure

Aesthetics

Affection

Affluence

Aggressiveness

Agility

Alertness

Altruism

Ambition

Amusement

Analytical
   thinking

Anticipation

Appreciation

Approachability

Approval

Art

Articulacy

Artistry

Assertiveness

Assurance

Attentiveness

Attractiveness

Audacity

Autonomy

Awareness

Awe

Balance

Beauty

Being the best

Belonging

Benevolence

Big-picture
   thinking

Bliss

Boldness

Brainstorming

Bravery

Brilliance

Calm

Calm under fire

Camaraderie

Candor

Capability

Care

Carefulness

Casualness

Celebrity

Certainty

Challenge

Change

Charisma

Charity	Consistency	Desire
Charm	Contentment	Determination
Cheerfulness	Continuity	Devotion
Clarity	Contribution	Devoutness
Cleanliness	Control	Dexterity
Clear-mindedness	Conversation	Dignity
Cleverness	Conviction	Diligence
Closeness	Cooperation	Diplomacy
Collaboration	Cordiality	Directness
Comfort	Correctness	Discipline
Commitment	Courage	Discovery
Common sense	Courtesy	Discretion
Communication	Craftiness	Diversity
Community	Creativity	Dominance
Compassion	Credibility	Dreaming
Competence	Cunning	Drive
Competitiveness	Curiosity	Duty
Completion	Daring	Eagerness
Composure	Decisiveness	Ease
Concentration	Decorum	Economy
Confidence	Dedication	Education
Conformity	Deference	Effectiveness
Congruency	Delight	Efficiency
Connection	Dependability	Elation
Consciousness	Depth	Elegance

Empathy	Fast thinking	Gratitude
Encouragement	Fearlessness	Gregariousness
Endurance	Ferocity	Growth
Energy	Fidelity	Guidance
Enjoyment	Fierceness	Happiness
Entertainment	Financial	Harmony
Enthusiasm	autonomy	Health
Ethics	Firmness	Heart
Euphoria	Fitness	Helpfulness
Excellence	Flexibility	Heroism
Excitement	Flow	Holiness
Exhilaration	Fluency	Honesty
Expediency	Focus	Honor
Experience	Fortitude	Hopefulness
Expertise	Frankness	Hospitality
Exploration	Freedom	Humility
Expressiveness	Friendliness	Humor
Extravagance	Friendship	Imagination
Extroversion	Frugality	Impact
Exuberance	Fun	Impartiality
Fairness	Gallantry	Independence
Faith	Generosity	Individuality
Fame	Gentility	Industry
Family	Giving	Influence
Fascination	Grace	Ingenuity

Inquisitiveness	Longevity	Outlandishness
Insightfulness	Love	Outrageousness
Inspiration	Loyalty	Partnership
Integrity	Majesty	Patience
Intellect	Marriage	Passion
Intelligence	Mastery	Peace
Intensity	Maturity	Perceptiveness
Intimacy	Meaning	Perfection
Introspection	Meekness	Perkiness
Intuition	Mellowness	Perseverance
Intuitiveness	Mentoring	Persistence
Inventiveness	Meticulousness	Personal growth
Investing	Mindfulness	Persuasiveness
Involvement	Modesty	Philanthropy
Joy	Motivation	Piety
Justice	Nature	Planning
Kindness	Neatness	Playfulness
Knowledge	Nonconformity	Pleasantness
Law and order	Obedience	Pleasure
Leadership	Open-mindedness	Poise
Learning	Openness	Polish
Liberty	Optimism	Popularity
Lightness	Order	Potency
Liveliness	Organization	Power
Logic	Originality	Practicality

Pragmatism	Resilience	Serenity
Precision	Resolution	Service
Preparedness	Resolve	Sharing
Presence	Resourcefulness	Shrewdness
Pride	Respect	Significance
Privacy	Responsibility	Silence
Proactivity	Rest	Silliness
Problem-solving	Restraint	Simplicity
Professionalism	Reverence	Sincerity
Prosperity	Richness	Skillfulness
Prudence	Rigor	Solidarity
Punctuality	Risk-taking	Solitude
Purity	Sacredness	Sophistication
Rationality	Sacrifice	Speed
Realism	Saintliness	Spirit
Reason	Satisfaction	Spirituality
Reasonableness	Science	Spontaneity
Recognition	Security	Stability
Recreation	Self-control	Status
Refinement	Self-expression	Status quo
Reflection	Selflessness	Stealth
Relaxation	Self-reliance	Stillness
Reliability	Self-respect	Strategic thinking
Religiousness	Sense of humor	Strength
Reputation	Sensitivity	Structure

Substance	Unflappability
Success	Uniqueness
Support	Unity
Supremacy	Usefulness
Surprise	Utility
Sympathy	Variety
Synergy	Victory
Teaching	Vigor
Teamwork	Virtue
Temperance	Vision
Tenacity	Vitality
Thankfulness	Vivacity
Thoroughness	Volunteering
Thoughtfulness	Warmhearted
Thrift	Warmth
Tidiness	Watchfulness
Timeliness	Wealth
Traditionalism	Willfulness
Tranquility	Willingness
Transcendence	Winning
Transparency	Wisdom
Trust	Wit
Trustworthiness	Worthiness
Truth	Youthfulness
Understanding	

APPENDIX B

	Level 1	Level 2	Level 3			
Sample Values Vault						
Value	DNA	Life-story	Dis-covered	Total	Peak Moment	Power Value

Bring together your DNA Values, Life-Story Values, and Discovered Values lists to create your Values Vault. I find it easier to list them alphabetically so I don't repeat a value.

Remember, a Power Value is one you have empowered. As you fill your Values Vault, note at what levels a value appears and the number of times it appears in each level. The more often it appears the more powerful it likely is in your work and life.

Look for *alike values* that have the same meaning for you. An example is dedication and persistence. If you feel they are different, keep them apart; otherwise put them together in your Values Vault and combine the number of times they were mined as one.

The number of times a value appears in your mining exercises indicates how often it is currently prevalent in your work and life. If it appears many times, it could be a value that is on automatic pilot, as discussed in chapter 4, "Name Your Values." If you find that it disconnects you, be more conscious about using it.

If a value is mined once or twice, there is opportunity to use it more often to broaden your ability to authentically connect with coworkers and broaden possibilities in your career by expanding your perspectives with a new Power Value.

Your Values Vault is your go-to source for the values you have discovered and can use in creating authentic connections.

Sample Values Vault:

Sample Values Vault						
	Level 1	Level 2	Level 3			
Value	DNA	Life-story	Dis-covered	Total	Peak Moment	Power Value
Focus	1	3	2	6	Baseball seams	✓
Trust	1	2	2	5	Comfort in chaos	✓
Simplicity	x	1	1	2	Fishing	✓
Freedom	x	3	1	4		
Organization	1	2	3	6		

APPENDIX C

	DNA Values List
1	
2	
3	
4	
5	
6	
7	
8	
9	
10	
11	
12	

APPENDIX D

Copy this page as many times as needed to list all the values you mine.

Life-Story Values List	
Value	Number of Times Mined

APPENDIX E

Copy this page as many times as needed to list all the values you mine.

Discovered Values List	
Value	Number of Times Mined

APPENDIX F

Goals and Challenges Worksheet	
Goals	Values
1.	
2.	
3.	
Challenges	Values
1.	
2.	
3.	

Highlight each goal and challenge with a sentence that envisions the big picture you want to achieve. Place the values you have chosen to empower next to it.

Examples:

- Goal: To increase my sales volume 25 percent in the next quarter.

- Values: Leadership, Listening, Confidence, Support

- Challenge: To enjoy my working relationship with John Doe.

- Values: Empathy, Friendship, Trust, Communication

APPENDIX G
POWER VALUES LIST

This is your Power Values List to practice with every day, embracing each value to be able to quickly and easily connect to it. I use a mnemonic to remind myself of my Power Values. For example, FEED = Focus, Enthusiasm, Enrollment, Discovery (see example on the next page). Your mnemonic can expand into a sentence as you increase the number of your Power Values. Create new mnemonics for new Power Values, and with practice you will own them.

Power Values List			
Mnemonic	Value	Peak Moment	Trigger

	Sample Power Values List		
Mnemonic	Value	Peak Moment	Trigger
F	Focus	Baseball seams	Eyes open
E	Enthusiasm	Skip to school	Thumbs up
E	Enrollment	King Kong in Van	Stand strong
D	Discovery	China market	Hand to eyebrow
W	Wisdom	Power question	Head raised to sky
E	Empathy	Mom's hand	Hand to shoulder
L	Listening	Between the lines	Hand to ear

APPENDIX H
POWER VALUES WORKSHEET

(See "An Example of the Steps to Empower and Connect to a Value" on page 87.)

Value: _____

Step 1 (exercise #12)

    Understand – free write

    Definition

    Serve me

Step 2 (exercise 13)

    Locate a value-empowering peak moment

    Body sensations

Step 3 (exercise 14)

    Empower the value

Step 4 (exercise 17)

    Connection trigger

APPENDIX I

Coworker's Values List		
Name:		
Value	Match	Not Match

REFERENCES

The 7 Hidden Reasons Employees Leave by Leigh Branham, Amacom Books, 2012.

Mastery: The Keys to Success and Long-Term Fulfillment by George Leonard, Plume, 1992.

"25 Years of Learning and Laughter" by Bill Gates, 2016: https://www.gatesnotes.com/About-Bill-Gates/25-Years-of-Learning-and-Laughter

INDEX

ABOUT THE AUTHOR

Barney Feinberg began his career as a CPA learning the language of business. At the age of twenty-five his career journey took him to live in Asia for seven years, where he was the COO of a buying office for a large clothing conglomerate. There he learned how to assimilate into a multitude of cultures, always with the purpose of building strong relationships at work.

His career in executive placement began in 1994. In 2002 he became a certified life coach with The Coaches Training Institute. He is a member of the International Coaching Federation with a Professional Co-Active Coach (PCC) distinction.

Barney began to merge his skills in recruiting and coaching, forming Life Balance Recruiting in 2006. This company evolved to become The Chemistry Factor, an executive coaching and recruiting organization. As he continued to develop his business model it became crystal clear to him that the most important factor for greater success in any job is the chemistry you have with the people you work with.

Barney is always open for new adventures and enjoys tennis, travel, and cooking. He has lived and worked in the New York City metropolitan area for the last thirty years.